JOURNAL FOR THE STUDY OF THE OLD TESTAMENT
SUPPLEMENT SERIES

414

Editors
Claudia V. Camp, Texas Christian University
and
Andrew Mein, Westcott House, Cambridge

Founding Editors
David J.A. Clines, Philip R. Davies and David M. Gunn

Editorial Board
Richard J. Coggins, Alan Cooper, John Goldingay,
Robert P. Gordon, Norman K. Gottwald, John Jarick,
Andrew D.H. Mayes, Carol Meyers, Patrick D. Miller

The Development and Symbolism of Passover until 70 CE

Tamara Prosic

T & T CLARK INTERNATIONAL
A Continuum imprint
LONDON • NEW YORK

Copyright © 2004 T&T Clark International
A Continuum imprint

Published by T&T Clark International
The Tower Building, 11 York Road, London, SE1 7NX
15 East 26th Street, Suite 1703, New York, NY 10010

www.tandtclark.com

British Library Cataloguing-in-Publication Data
A catalogue record for this book is available from the British Library.

ISBN 0-8264-7087-4 (hardback)

Typeset by Data Standards Ltd, Frome, Somerset BA11 1RE
Printed on acid-free paper in Great Britain by MPG Books Ltd, Bodmin,
Cornwall

CONTENTS

PREFACE

The problems of Passover's development and meaning have been a subject of considerable interest in a variety of academic disciplines. They have been discussed by biblical scholars, historians of religion, anthropologists and archaeologists. Most studies, however, were carried out before the recent developments in explaining the early history of the Israelites and thus also their cultural origins, a fact that has considerably burdened my attempts to find recent discussions on the topic, in particular the ones reflective of the new historical paradigm in explaining the origins of the Israelites.

Quoted biblical texts and references are from the Revised Standard Version. Certain parts of the dissertation were published in an abridged form as articles: 'Passover in Biblical Narratives', *Journal for the Study of the Old Testament* 82 (1999), pp. 45–55; 'Origin of Passover', *Scandinavian Journal of the Old Testament* 13 (1999), pp. 78–94.

ACKNOWLEDGEMENTS

This study is a revision of my PhD dissertation which I submitted at the University of Melbourne in 2004. Many events, good and bad, stood in the way of completing it. Each of them brought a particular emotional turmoil that took my mind away from Passover, and from which it took some time to recover and re-focus. However, they were not just time-consuming and distracting affairs. Some of those experiences actually opened my eyes to the importance of particular dimensions and realities of life that subsequently helped me understand some of the aspects of Passover.

The bombardment of my native country Yugoslavia in 1999 and the loss of a close family member almost made me give up working on the thesis because at the time it seemed that the pen could never be mightier than the sword and that every intellectual endeavour was merely a self-indulgence. But, then it also made me think of powers that are beyond reach, of their volatile character and possible ways of controlling that volatility, ideas that much later proved crucial in understanding the overall purpose of Passover. The birth of my son Lazar and his hungry cries, on the other hand, reminded me of how enormously important is the physical side of our existence and how vital it is to have enough food to stop the cravings of the body, a thing that can be so easily forgotten in today's western societies with such an abundance of food, but which was of major importance to ancient cultures.

For undivided support during these very turbulent years of my life I wish to express my gratitude to Associate Professor Dr Ziva Shavitsky, my supervisor, who through formal and informal discussions has assisted me both professionally and personally. This work could not have been possible without the Australian Postgraduate Award which I received during the preparation of the dissertation. For that and for the understanding they showed by approving every leave of absence that I requested I am especially indebted to the staff of the School of Graduate Studies at the University of Melbourne.

I am particularly grateful to my friend Olga Vujovic, who went through a painstaking process of correcting my English and editing the final draft of the dissertation.

My gratitude also goes to everyone who has asked me, with a spark of real interest, 'How is it going?' My greatest indebtedness, however, is to the members of my family. Those far away from me, my parents, for their love and unwavering trust. And those near me, my very 'new-age' husband who willingly and lovingly took over a mammoth share of the domestic chores and parenting responsibilities and who always had the time to discuss Passover with me; my older son Eli, who patiently waited to be allowed to play his games on the 'better computer'; and finally Lazar, who waited to become a 'big boy' and stop using nappies. Without them this work would not be possible and as much as it is mine it is theirs as well.

Introduction

Before the destruction of the Jerusalem temple in 70 CE effectively eliminated temple worship and in many ways fundamentally changed the ritual form in which the majority of Yahweh's followers honoured and celebrated their god, one of the requirements of his cult was a triple journey to the temple in order to collectively participate in the performance of the three annual festivals, Passover, Weeks and Tabernacles. Among them, Passover is the only one that is traditionally regarded as embedded in two different cultural traditions and whose function and symbolic references are interpreted from two different perspectives. This study intends to challenge that habitually accepted conjecture and demonstrate that the new historical paradigm regarding the cultural origins of the biblical Israelites opens up the possibility for a more consequential interpretation of the festival, both with respect to its ritual organization and its meaning.

The study opens with a chapter that gives a brief review of the current trends in interpreting the early history and religion of the Israelites and a discussion regarding the method of reading the biblical text employed in this work. These wider theoretical and methodological considerations are followed by a presentation of Passover theories, the main purpose of which is to display the variety and inconsistency of scholarly conclusions regarding the festival's development and its function.

The second part of the study analyses the most frequently used arguments in support of the dual origins theory. Questions such as the effects of the centralization, the alleged family and/or pastoral nature of the Passover sacrifice as opposed to the temple and/or agricultural character of the Feast of the Unleavened Bread are tested against the biblical texts themselves and against the wider background of socio-economic conditions and the cultural and religious traditions of the ancient Near East. This part also includes a discussion on theories that view Passover as a single festival, but expound the hypothesis that its function in times before it became the centrepiece of the salvation history was primarily in relation to the calendar rather than the season in which it took place.

The concluding part of the book deals with the festival's symbolism. The discussion opens with an analysis of biblical narratives which mention Passover celebrations. The analysis has been conducted in a structuralist manner, primarily because it attempts to establish the fundamental constants behind the level of phenomenal appearances and perceptible intentions. This general determination of Passover's symbolism is followed by discussion regarding its time organization. Two different aspects have been considered. The symbolic references of the season in which the festival takes place and the meaning of the particular time structure of the two known rituals. The time symbolism is followed by investigation of the symbolic references of individual elements of the ritual during the first night of Passover, such as the vigil, the eating, the sacrificial animal and the treatment of the bones.

PART I

Chapter 1

SOME THEORETICAL AND METHODOLOGICAL CONSIDERATIONS

1.1. *Wider Theoretical Premises*

Every attempt to trace the development of the Israelite religion or any of its rituals in many ways depends and relies on the accepted theoretical position with respect to the wider historical problems related to the origins of the Israelites and the pre-monarchic history. Passover studies are no exception in this respect and in some cases the conclusions regarding the festival's nature and origins come as direct ramification of the espoused view regarding the cultural and ethnic origins of the Israelites. Given that dependence it is felt necessary to include as part of this study the historical views which this study takes as its initial premise.

The majority of theories on Passover are built on the assumption that the ancient Israelites were ethnic foreigners, nomads, who either by force or by peaceful infiltration settled in the land of Canaan. The assumption is based on the biblical understanding of the early Israelites, and in terms of its value as a cornerstone upon which other theories can be built is of questionable value since it still awaits some non-biblical, external, archaeological evidence to surface and substantiate it. In recent decades scholars interested in these more encompassing historical problems acknowledged the existing inconsistency between the biblical views and the picture painted by non-biblical evidence, and the understanding of both the biblical traditions and the early history of Israel has shifted significantly. The previous almost uncontested authority of the Bible in matters related to the ancient history of Palestine has gradually eroded, reaching today the stage of almost complete distrust. Rather than being regarded as testimonies of the times they purport to describe and taken at face value, the biblical traditions are comprehended by an ever increasing number of scholars as stories with an ideological purpose of advancing the theological or political agenda of their authors.[1]

Several closely related arguments have been put forward as reasons for rejecting them as a credible source for historical research. First, the versions which came to us are at best second-hand ones since they were

---

1. Lemche 1988: 53–54; Garbini 1988: 14–17; Davies 1992: 116–20.

completed in a much later period of Israel's history than the portrayed events.[2] Second, because the intention behind compiling the Old Testament was not to describe the secular, but the religious history of Israel.[3] And finally, because even that religious history is given from the perspective of the prevailing worldview at the time of its final redaction.[4] According to N.P. Lemche, when these facts are acknowledged, it must be concluded that these traditions primarily reflect concerns and ideas of the period in which they arose, and only secondarily tell something about events from an earlier period which they may claim to describe.[5] As a result of this shift in understanding the Bible and the increased reliance on non-biblical evidence in reconstructing the socio-economic, cultural and political history of ancient Palestine, completely new interpretations of the origins and the early history of Israel have appeared.

Acknowledging the impossibility of reconciling the archaeological evidence from Palestine with the biblical representation of the Israelite settlement in Canaan, one of the very first among the traditional views about the ancient Israelites to be found problematic and subsequently rejected was the one about their intrusion into Palestine and their separate ethnic origins from that of the indigenous population of Palestine, the infamous biblical Canaanites. New ideas have appeared as to who were really the biblical Israelites and what was the true nature of the antagonism portrayed in the Bible as an inter-ethnic conflict between Israelites and Canaanites. The literature that this complex debate produced is too immense to be reviewed here. For the purposes of this work it will suffice to say that the latest view on the matter is that the biblical differentiation between Israelites and Canaanites was an ideologically motivated invention in order to designate the followers of the true god and those of the false gods.

Along with the idea about Israelite separate ethnic origins, many other biblically based and previously unquestioned views, such as the early monotheistic nature of Yahwism, have been revised and modified. According to the picture painted by non-biblical sources, Yahweh was worshipped alongside other deities[6] and there are indications that the polytheistic cults continued well into the Persian period.[7]

The development of Yahwistic monotheism is also viewed from a different perspective. Contrary to the belief that it was a very early development and more or less a matter of sudden introduction, Thompson, Edelman, Lemche and others regard it as a long and complex

2. Lemche 1988: 39–40; 25–30; also Davies 1992: 94–112; Thompson 1994: 88–112.
3. Lemche 1988: 30; Garbini 1988: 14.
4. Davies 1992: 116–18.
5. Lemche 1988: 55; Thompson 1999: 62–81.
6. See the comprehensive works of Keel and Uehlinger 1998, Wyatt 2000 and Zevit 2001.
7. Van der Toorn 1992: 80–101.

historical process the beginnings of which can be recognized in the increase of Assyrian imperial influences on religious thought[8] and in the monopolization process in which certain gods gain in importance and sometimes completely absorb the functions and identities of other gods.[9] According to Thompson, Yahwism with monotheistic tendencies developed as a regionalized version of a world-view and particular understanding of the transcendent shared by the contingent cultures from the Western Mediterranean to the Indus valley and from Anatolia to the Sudan.[10] The dominant characteristic of this changed world-view was not rejection of previous traditions, but rather their reinterpretation and restructuring.[11] As Thompson says, 'They rather reflected different aspects of a common spectrum of intellectual development. There was continuity between polytheism and monotheism as well as a process of changing interpretation. Hardly sudden or revolutionary, the changes of worldview were the result of more than a millennium of cultural integration.'[12] Under the Persians and their policy of equating the head deities of national pantheons with Ahura Mazda under the new abstract title 'godhead of the heavens', Yahwism initially developed as an 'inclusive monotheism' that translates and recasts polytheistic conceptions through universalistic terms.[13] At some stage during the Hellenistic period, the inclusive Yahwism was transformed into exclusive monotheism that rejected the existence of multiple manifestations of the head deity and concentrated only on the existence of a single male creator deity: Yahweh.[14] This kind of monotheism found its full expression in the official religion during the short period of the Hasmonean state.

However, it seems that scholars have yet to fully understand the importance of these new trends in interpreting Israelite early history and religion and the bearings they have on theories regarding their religious practice. The slowness in embracing the new historical paradigm as a wider theoretical framework has been particularly prominent in interpreting individual elements of the Israelite cultic worship, such as the meaning of festivals and rituals. Explanations of Passover ritual characteristics, for example, are still permeated with concepts such as nomadism, pastoralism, syncretism, tribalism and the like that are inherited from the old academic view which understood the ancient Israelite culture and religion as crucially and irreconcilably different from those of the Canaanites.

8.   Thompson 1999: 380–81.
9.   Lemche 1998: 217–18.
10.   Thompson 1995: 111.
11.   Thompson 1995: 114–16.
12.   Thompson 1999: 381.
13.   Edelman 1995: 22.
14.   Edelman 1995: 23.

For the studies of Passover the changed view on the origins of the Israelites is an extremely important development because it opens a completely new interpretative angle, especially when it comes to questions such as its function prior to the historicization and the dual cultural source of its rituals. In contrast to the old historical model whose view on the ethnic and cultural origins of the Israelites reflected in studies of Passover as a search for distinctiveness and separate functional entities in its ritual structure, the new trends provide a basis for an assumption that the festival comes from a single cultural background and that it is, despite our inability to understand the governing idea behind it, a coherent unit, both ritually and functionally. It justifies and encourages searching for the commonalities and the unifying elements behind the differences of the biblical representations of the festival.

Of particular significance is also the understanding that between the early polytheistic religion and the exclusive Yahwism of the Hellenistic period there was an interim form of Yahwism that was not antagonistic towards polytheism. Such a notion provides a more operative framework within which the cultic practice related by the biblical texts can be investigated given that the religious tradition reflected in many of the books of the Old Testament is also neither polytheistic nor strictly monotheistic, but most of the time somewhere in between. Its best description would be a monotheism in flux, a monotheism that still strives to define and establish its exclusiveness. The idea of inclusive Yahwism, as a form of monotheism that rather than rejecting previous religious traditions tended to reinterpret them, opens up the possibility that the religious symbolic references of the biblical texts, including those of Passover, are closer to the polytheistic understanding of the world than they might appear on the surface. Such assimilative religious context allows perusal and interpretation of Passover's symbolism that go beyond the festival's declared historical and commemorative meaning. In this study, the offered interpretation of Passover's development and symbolism both draws and builds its argumentation on the two aforementioned theoretical developments.

1.2. *Methodological Problems*

In discussing Passover we shall consult a variety of textual sources such as the writings of Philo, Josephus, the tractates of the Mishnah, the Ugaritic cycle of myths, and so on. However, as in any other study of early Israelite religion, the main body of texts on which we shall rely for information about its development and from which we shall derive comparable metaphors and symbolical references will come from the Old Testament. Given the mentioned shift in the scholarly attitude towards the credibility of biblical texts as historical documents, and that answers regarding

Passover's pre-commemorative function and its origins suggest research with historical ambitions, it is necessary to say a few words about the methodological approach that we intend to implement in this study. In the case of Passover establishing an effective methodological framework is particularly important considering that the festival is mentioned in various parts of the Old Testament and in complex texts that are thematically and stylistically very different. References to the festival can be encountered as part of writings with a clear narrative function, but also as part of the legislative corpus, in instructions, lists and laws. This diversity clearly demands an explanation with respect to the method that will be employed in order to extract useful historical data from the mentioned references.

In scholarly readings there are in principle two methods of approaching the contents of the biblical texts. The diachronic approach treats the element of its interest in a developmental way, as part of the historical process and dynamics, while the synchronic disregards the progressive side and views the element within a certain delineated textual, historical, cultural or other system. In theory and when they are a subject of definition it is quite easy to distinguish between the two methods. However, when it comes to their practical application, very frequently scholars digress from the straight path of one or the other. Such methodological inconsistency, on the other hand, is not so much a result of scholarly incompetence or carelessness in consequently applying one or the other method as much as it is a matter of spontaneous surrender to the peculiar character of the Old Testament. The indiscriminate use of diverse literary styles, blending of genres and themes make the biblical text not only a very distinct, but also an unusually hard and demanding work for reading. In attempting to convey the external complexity of the biblical text and the need for an interpretative stance in its reading, Northrop Frye called it the great code.[15] And he was certainly right because the Bible has all the characteristics of an encoded message that requires special keys to unlock its meaning. However, in contrast to other coded texts for which there is usually only one way of decoding that in turn brings to light a single, unvarying rendering, the biblical code seems to have the quality of being an open code, very much in line with U. Eco's qualification of art works as open works,[16] to which a variety of interpretative keys can be applied resulting in different messages and meanings. Therefore it is possible to read the Genesis story about Terah, Abraham, Ur and Haran as folk aetiologies expressing 'Helenism's belief in the common origin and universal quality of humanity, in spite of its obvious diversity',[17] but also as a politically opportune fabrication on behalf of the exiled Israelites

15. Frye 1982.
16. Eco 1989.
17. Thompson 1999: 40.

seeking a favourable position during the reign of Nabonidus, the Babylonian king, whose preferred god Sin had his principal seats precisely in Ur and Haran.[18] T. Thompson used the function of the story as the key for his interpretation, while G. Garbini used the 'Sitz im Leben' key, that is the specific historical and political circumstances in which the story could have been born.

This openness to manifold interpretations, on the other hand, is not an intended, self-conscious result or choice of the creative minds that participated in the formation of the biblical writings. Its main creator and contributor is actually the fact that what we know about the historical and socio-cultural circumstances surrounding their formation is infinitely small in comparison with what we do not know. What we can state with absolute certainty is that the Old Testament's formation was a complex process involving a variety of cultural, political and historical strands.[19] Answers as to the temporal and the geographical origins of the traditions as well as the identity of the author(s)[20] and the audience for which the writings were originally intended[21] are still shrouded in complete darkness and a matter of ongoing debate. And it is these unsettled questions as to the who, when, where, why, for whom and in which circumstances parts of the Old Testament were composed that opens the potential for nearly endless interpretations.

From the perspective of that almost non-existent knowledge about its formation, the Old Testament, with its different traditions, obsessive repetitions, contradictory versions of the same events, inconsistent genealogies and chronologies, mythologized history and historicized myths, poems, sayings, laws, and so on, externally mostly resembles a collage, a particular form of art in which the final outcome is the result of bringing together and re-using bits and pieces of different purpose, origin, texture, and so on, as semantic and structural components of a new complex whole. With respect to its components and their interpretation, collage, however, allows only the synchronic perspective, the dynamism of which happens in the interplay of its own elements, within its own system encapsulated in the moment of the artist's intention. It is essentially two-dimensional, the dimensions being here and now. The significance and the cognitive value of the re-used material is entirely dependent on the synchronic structure of the new semantic whole. In other words, collage disassociates its components from their previous history, and questions that refer to their past such as the origins of a piece of glass glued to the canvas, whether it comes from a window or from a bottle, who was the

18. Garbini 1988: 77–79.
19. Davies 1992; Thompson 1999.
20. Were they the 73 sages of the Septuagint or the Palestinian priests and scribes?
21. Was it written for the Palestinian Jews or the diaspora?

manufacturer, and so on, are absurd because they do not contribute in any way to the attempt to understand their semantics within the context of the new whole.

The Old Testament to a large extent shares this two-dimensional, here and now, synchronic feature of artistic collages, and in this sense E. Leach is right when he says that the entire biblical text is synchronic, that 'there is no development, only dialectical inversion'.[22] However, while an art collage never inspires questions that go beyond the synchronic picture, the biblical collage is continuously subjected to inquiries with historical overtones. Scholars want to know about the origins of its traditions and the socio-political, intellectual and religious developments influential in their formation before they were permanently fixed on the canvas titled the Old Testament. Such distinctly different scholarly interest brings to the forefront the question of the *differentia specifica* of the biblical collage in contrast to the artistic one.

As mentioned earlier, in an artistic collage the meaning and the interrelatedness of its individual components depend solely on the semantics of the new whole. The relationship between the collage as a whole and its elements is one of internal holonymy. In the biblical collage, however, the existence of such internal 'whole to part relation' is highly questionable. Despite the commonly held notion that the components of the biblical pastiche are held together by some dominant ideological or theological idea, it is actually impossible to identify any underlying motivation that would be able to explain every inconsistency or anomaly of the biblical text. As Thompson argues, 'the pluralism of our text is so obvious' that 'whatever the "tradition as a whole" may be, it must be recognised as the tradition we have – and this does not display the theologically motivated ideology commonly asserted to it'.[23] It is mostly this inability to clearly distinguish the inherent 'dominant semantic whole' to which all individual elements of the Old Testament could be meaningfully related that is responsible for the obsession of biblical scholarship with historical research. What scholars are actually trying to do by treating the biblical text in a diachronic way is to substitute the missing theologically or otherwise motivated encompassing whole with semantic wholes from the domain of history. It is a pursuit for the 'whole to part relationship' to which the biblical pieces once belonged and which can act as their explanans. In our research of Passover we shall also engage in pursuit of the semantic wholes that can meaningfully explain the inconsistencies in its biblical representations. However, in doing so we shall keep in mind that in order to claim that any of those inconsistencies reflect a real historical development we need to have a supporting

22. Leach 1980: 76–77.
23. Thompson 1994: 369–71.

historical context. That historical context, on the other hand, cannot come from the biblical stories purporting to be history. It has to be found outside the biblical world and based on the existing factual knowledge of the history and the conditions of the ancient Near East.

Finding such an external control, on the other hand, might seem an altogether impossible task given that the general perception is that specifically Israelite non-biblical historical and cultural points of reference for the changes in the cult are either completely missing or are dishearteningly insufficient. However, this perception has to do more with our unwitting acceptance of the biblical views than with our knowledge about real ancient Israel. Instead of being aware that the Old Testament is a book that represents the world and history from a very biased religious point of view, most frequently we take for granted that non-Yahwistic practices such as the adoration of Baal or other deities to which the Bible refers were not originally Israelite because the writings themselves qualify them as serving foreign gods. We tend to forget that from the viewpoint of Yahwistic theology everything that is not condoned by Yahweh is foreign.[24] When this ideological trap into which the Bible can lure us is combined with the scarce archaeological finds of longer written documents from Palestine, the conviction that, apart from what can be read in the Bible, it is not possible to know more about the specific Israelite religion, only becomes stronger. In a sense, this persuasion is not that far from the truth. However, not because the evidence is completely missing, as the Bible would have us believe, but because there never really was a unique ancient Israelite religion. Nor was there the biblical Israel as the latest theories in studies of early Israelite history claim.[25] Their main assertion is that such an Israel as is portrayed in the Bible came into existence only in post-exilic times and only as an ideological literary construct. As mentioned earlier, according to growing numbers of scholars the ethnic and cultural differences between the Israelites and the indigenous population of Palestine, the biblical Canaanites, advocated by the biblical view, is artificial and should be eliminated. The archaeological artefacts, as scanty as they may be, also support this latest interpretation because nothing that can be identified as particularly Israelite has been found.[26] And the religion of those people, the occupants of what was later known as Yehud, the Persian province where Judaism as

---

24. Regarding the demagogical power of marking something as foreign, a very contemporary example can serve as a good illustration. In Australian politics labelling the policies of an opposing political party as being 'un-Australian' is a very frequently used verbal weapon. In this respect it is perhaps not without importance that Australia, similarly to the biblical Israel, still struggles to find the set of particular cultural values that could be defined as typically Australian.

25. Davies 1992; Thompson 1999.

26. Coote and Whitelam 1987: 125–26.

a monotheistic cult developed and where the biblical construct of Israel was born, reveals marked similarities to the religious traditions of their more powerful and richer neighbours who for their part left abundant evidence regarding their cultures.

The geographical position of ancient Israel and Judah was not a very fortunate place for either political or cultural development. Being between the rock and the hard place – the big powers of the ancient Near East, Egypt on one side and Assyria and later Babylon and Persia on the other – Palestine was the periphery, the border region of shifting alliances, never clearly defined and always a target whenever any of the real political and military powers wanted to extend their territories. The scantiness of archaeological evidence is certainly at least partially due to that almost constant warring and physical destruction to which the region and would-be cultural and political centres of Palestine were subjected. We should also perhaps take into consideration the religious zeal of Yahweh's priests who, once firmly established as the ruling authorities on issues of faith, were probably inclined to destroy everything that could be a reminder of other deities.[27] The dearth of impressive temples or palaces in Palestine that we can admire and that can conjure up for us an almost tangible context, and lack of archives from which we can directly learn about the particulars of the social organization and religious traditions of this region, does not thereby mean that the so-called Israelites were much different from their immediate neighbours. Their kinship was a very close one and involved more than just language. Palestine as a geographical region no doubt had its socio-cultural idiosyncrasies and they have to be taken into account, but, as Thompson says, they have to be understood as such 'within the greater context of this region, its politics and religions, as aspects of the history of Greater Syria'.[28] Our discussion regarding Passover will take this context of Greater Syria as the supporting historical context and cultural referent.

In discussing the questions related to its development we shall not be concerned with the chronology of the possible changes in its ritual structure. As far as the historical ambition of this work is concerned the only division into chronological periods that might prove operational is according to the changes at the ideological and functional level of Passover. That is, to periods before and after its transformation into a commemorative festival celebrating the exodus. Given that Passover holds a very central role in the Bible's ideology, the precise historical period in

---

27. Garbini suggests that the 3rd of Tishri, which in the Megilat Taanit is designated as the date when the memory of the documents was eliminated, perhaps refers to destruction of royal inscriptions and similar epigraphic evidence (Garbini 1988: 16–17). The destruction of the material remains of the reign of Amenophis IV is another good example of how a religious animosity can be very successful in producing a lack of archaeological data.

28. Thompson 1997: 183; Lemche 1997: 131–32; Garbini 1988: 2.

which the redefinition of its function took place cannot be determined. What we can firmly establish in those terms is not the earliest period, *terminus a quo*, but the *terminus ad quem* of that change. Even dating of that *terminus ad quem* is relative since it depends on the period when the biblical texts were finally written. If we accept the latest studies regarding this question, that may be as late as Hellenistic times.[29] So what we could possibly establish in historical terms is that Passover's ideological and corresponding functional translation is evident in Hellenistic times, but how far back into the past from the fourth or the third century that process started it is not possible to say. The problem of chronology becomes even more complicated if we take into account the possibility that there was a difference between the official and the popular understanding of the festival. Popular beliefs are very deeply rooted and it may have taken several generations before the official and the popular interpretation synchronized. Our main 'historical' interest therefore will not be in establishing exact dates or periods in which Passover changes took place, but the possible effects that certain historically confirmed trends in the development of the cult or certain historical events might have had on the ritual structure of Passover. More concretely, we shall deal with the idea of centralization as reflected in Deuteronomy and attempt to answer whether the trend to centralize the cult could have had some effect on Passover, but we shall leave aside specific questions such as the date when the first centralized observance took place. The important thing will be that as a general tendency the centralization of the cult is historically confirmed, given that in times immediately before the second destruction of the temple, its practical implementation has largely been realized, and that as such it provides a supporting historical context for some of the ideas expressed in the book of Deuteronomy.

The discussion regarding the dual origins and pre-commemorative function of Passover will be mainly based on analyses of the representation of the festival in the legislative texts. Given that ordinances possess an inherently rigid nature, in particular if regarded as being ordained by divine authority, we thought it reasonable to assume that they might reflect a certain reality or at least an anticipated reality. In our investigation they will be regarded as possibly diachronic and indicative of the changes in the Passover ritual. Without attempting to place them into any particular historical period or to establish their chronological order, they will be analysed in order to establish whether there are constant elements that can indicate some continuum in form, but also to determine the variable elements that could be a result of known historical developments. Other biblical texts in which celebrations of Passover feature as part of a story, given that stories in general are much more flexible and more open

29.   Lemche 1993: 163–93; Thompson 1999.

to a variety of different influences, will be considered basically as synchronic and ahistorical. This division, on the other hand, should be considered as provisional since these two kinds of texts are sometimes in their original biblical version very closely intertwined. That is particularly the case with the texts from the Pentateuch where the laws are mostly presented within the context of some important event. While it is possible for the sake of methodological consistency to distinguish between legislative and storytelling literary styles, we must be cautious against interpreting them without taking into account the larger textual framework because they involve different discourse patterns and coexistence of both diachronic and synchronic meanings.

It is clear from everything stated that our way of attempting to trace possible modifications and developments in Passover's ritual will significantly digress from the almost routine path of source criticism that is followed by similar studies in biblical scholarship. Such an aberrant position requires explanation, especially because the majority of theories advocating Passover's dual origins that we shall review and most often dispute as part of our research relied solely on the source hypothesis as a theoretical basis.

Until recently, source criticism was almost unanimously accepted as the most reliable method to deduce some definite conclusions about the development of the Israelite religious practice. The four sources[30] of the Pentateuch were thought to originate from various periods in the history of the Israelites and as such were regarded also as being reflective of the religion of Israel in those periods.[31] The research mainly involved minute linguistic inspection and comparison of the descriptions of the cult as given in the different sources. As a method that investigates the growth of the Pentateuch, source criticism has greatly contributed to the understanding of the complex dynamics involved in the formation process itself. However, as a historical method, supposed to clarify the development of the cult, it has serious shortcomings, and a number of reasons argue against it in reading and interpreting the biblical texts. Its main fallacy in this respect is the assumed correlation between biblical texts and certain periods in the history of Israel, which is based solely on linguistic criteria for which there is almost no external control. There are no non-biblical

30. The generally accepted notion is that four distinctive sources contributed to the formation of the Old Testament. Namely, the Yahwistic (J), the Deuteronomic (D), the Elohistic (E) and the Priestly tradition (P). J is supposed to originate from the period of early monarchy c. 950 BCE and its main characteristic is the preference of the name Yahweh. E is supposed to come from the north and prefers Elohim as a divine name. It is dated c. 850 BCE. D is supposed to reflect the changes introduced by Josiah's religious reform in the seventh century BCE. P is supposed to be the latest, dating from the period of the Babylonian exile or after it, c. 550 BCE and later. Anderson 1978: 18–23.

31. De Vaux 1965: II, 484.

linguistic points of reference by which the biblical linguistic variations can be historically fixed.[32] In the case of Passover that means that J source, traditionally regarded as the oldest, cannot be taken with certainty to reflect the form that the observance of the festival had in the tenth century BCE as opposed to some later period. The appearance of well-argued theories claiming that J source originates from exilic times[33] undermines the very idea that it is possible to construct any chronology based on biblical linguistics. Another weakness of the source criticism is the lack of attention to the contextual meaning of the presumably source-specific phraseology. As J.B. Segal argued in his book on Passover, technical terms and phrases are not the 'stock-in-trade' of individual sources and are always employed as the context requires.[34] How unreliable the source criticism is as a historical method will be clear from the review of Passover theories. Although applied to the same texts, the method leads to a perplexing diversity of conclusions.

Rejecting the source criticism as a method for our research on the development of Passover does not mean that we deny the possibility that biblical texts referring to the festival originated from different historical periods or from different regions of Palestine. Variations in the texts regarding the structure of the festival are perhaps indications of changes or even of simultaneously existing different versions. But, in deciding whether they reflect a real change or not we shall take into account factors other than language, such as the role a particular piece of legislation plays in the wider narrative framework or whether a particular variation is consistent with some historical development that would foster it.

After the discussion regarding questions pertaining to its development we shall turn to a symbolic interpretation of the festival. Passover will be seen through the anthropological lenses that view ritual as a patterned, repetitive enactment of a cultural belief and value[35] through an assemblage of symbols clustered around the nucleus of dominant symbols.[36] It will be viewed as an action the nature of which is pragmatic, but also as a statement that communicates symbolic meanings. The biblical text will be treated in a synchronic way as the carrier of meanings that reach beyond the stated.

In dealing with Passover's semantic puzzle from which many and without any doubt important pieces are irretrievably lost, we shall have to employ what Eilberg-Schwartz calls 'cultural archeology, a mode of interpretation that involves imagining what practices meant from incom-

---

32.   Davies 1992: 105.
33.   Van Seters 1975; Schmid 1976.
34.   Segal 1963: 91.
35.   Davies-Floyd 1992: 8.
36.   Turner 1977: 186.

plete and partial remains'.[37] In order to substitute the missing pieces we shall also have to resort to cross-cultural studies that can 'point to meanings and functions of a practice only hinted at in the literary remains. Comparison thus emerges as a tool for imagining the unspoken meanings and correspondence that once constituted a cultural system.'[38]

One rare point on which scholars dealing with Passover unanimously agree is that the ritual was taken over from previous religious tradition. Similar to other pre-monotheistic elements that were incorporated into the new belief system, Passover's symbolic scope and references were also changed. However, as V. Turner suggests, 'new ritual items, even new ritual configurations, tend more often to be variants of old themes than radical novelties'.[39] In this respect, religious traditions and rituals are especially resilient cultural phenomena. They are never readily abandoned and the new theology usually inherits the outstanding moments, or as Turner would call them 'themes', of its immediate predecessor. That incorporation, sometimes only in a symbolic form, provides a continuum between the old and the new. As the thing that can be recognized and understood, it alleviates the burden of accepting the new theology; it negotiates the passage from the old to the new by being involved with both. To paraphrase E. Goodenough: theology is for few; symbols are for all, intellectuals and childish alike.[40] Examples for this claim are numerous and some of them are common knowledge. No anthropologist would interpret, for example, the symbolism of the Virgin Mary without drawing parallels with the ancient Great Mother. However, in many other cases the incorporation of the old is not immediately obvious. In time, around the symbolic kernel of the old tradition, new clusters of symbols grow. Initially related to the old religious milieu, they continue to develop within and in relation to the new theological interpretative framework which eventually might obscure or push into the background the old core. Due to the Yahwistic ideological redefinition, Passover is one of such cases and in attempting to meaningfully interpret some of its symbolic references we shall turn to ideas that are historically much older than the biblical texts.

Always closely related to the question of the meaning of a religious ritual is the question of myth. In the case of Passover this question cannot be overlooked because, in the Bible, Passover ritual is inseparable from a tale. We have the narrated and the performed, the myth, although in a

---

37. Eilberg-Schwartz 1990: 27.
38. Eilberg-Schwartz 1990: 27.
39. Turner 1977: 184.
40. Goodenough 1988: 49–51. Frazer's contemporary, R.R. Marrett, remarked in a similar vein that 'savage religion is something not so much thought out as danced out'. In Comstock 1971: 35.

historical disguise, and the ritual. The story in question is, of course, the exodus. With respect to the relation between the exodus and Passover our main concern will be to establish whether the tale, apart from its aetiological purpose, implicitly contains other messages about the festival.

Having outlined our approach to Passover in biblical writings it is necessary to critically position ourselves with respect to the main academic traditions that we will be drawing upon in our study, namely symbolic anthropology and biblical studies.

Apart from a few but nevertheless very inspiring works,[41] anthropologists have mainly abstained from interpreting the ancient Israelite religion. Among the many issues that play a role in this abstention,[42] the one that is by anthropologists themselves regarded as the most important one is the fragmentary and indirect nature of the sources. It has to be admitted that reconstructing something from fragments is a frustrating task and at best can claim to be only a tentative one. However, as contra argument, one could question the validity and the depth of insight into cultural complexities gained by typical anthropological methods, namely field observation or interview, which have their own frustrating limitations. How much can one really learn about certain culture through field work that is most often of very limited duration or by interviews that are done with only superficial knowledge of the language, if any? And what is the real value of the information 'It has always been like that', which is a reply anthropologists most often get from their informants, even if it is acquired first-hand. Such directly gained knowledge speaks a lot about the nature of traditions in general, that they do not have to be rationalized in order to be followed, but it does not say anything about their meaning. In that respect, it certainly says less than 'This day shall be for you a memorial day, and you shall keep it as a feast to the Lord; throughout your generations you shall observe it as an ordinance for ever.'[43] This sounds very much like a rationalization indicating that its purpose might be a reinterpretation of an old tradition.

In the refusal of anthropologists to deal with the ancient Israelite religion it seems that there is an underlying notion that biblical descriptions of ritual practices should somehow replace their real enactment. However, to treat biblical descriptions as if they were ethnographical reports is to make the same mistake as the historians who take biblical narratives at face value. They might be a very good indication, but very often the same ritual is differently described and it is

41. The works of Mary Douglas, *Purity and Danger*; Edmund Leach and D. Alan Aycock, *Structuralist Interpretation of the Biblical Myth*; and H. Eilberg-Schwartz, *The Savage in Judaism*.

42. H. Eilberg-Schwartz gives an excellent review of these issues. See Eilberg-Schwartz 1990: 31–67.

43. Exod. 12.14.

hard to establish which description is the most credible in terms of its live performance. The Bible is not an exemplary book when it comes to information and in that respect it can never replace notes taken in a live situation, but it is on the other hand a considerable resource with respect to what ultimately interests symbolic anthropology the most. It is a book laden with meanings. Frye named it the great code, Leach speaks about it as sacred history and in Garbini's, Thompson's and Davies' discussions it is treated as a retrojective ideological projection.[44] These qualifications illustrate that the content of biblical texts should be treated as semantic and interpretative rather than informative or descriptive. In this sense, the Bible is much better than any informant anthropologists can find and it is a pity that the rituals in the Bible and their meanings were mainly left to be interpreted by biblical scholars without the input of the anthropological perspective.

The biblical scholars, on the other hand, trying to find a way that will allow them to advance interpretation of the scriptures unencumbered by the dogmatism of the church, developed an overly positivistic method based on the language of the Bible. Their interpretations of the biblical rituals came as a result of very complicated etymological analyses of words and phrases, frequently taken out of context, which, however, in terms of their semantic side actually produced very little. What was put aside in scholarly pursuit of freedom of interpretation and scientific objectivity through linguistics is that the Bible is a sacred book and, like every other sacred book, its language is a symbolic, metaphorical language that more than it speaks through words speaks through unstated meanings.

In our research we shall try to meet ancient Passover on a middle ground between anthropology and biblical studies where it will be possible to include the results of both and enable their cross-fertilization, in the hope that we will achieve a more unified and comprehensive understanding of this festival.

1.3. *Theories about Passover*

The Israelites had three major annual festivals: Passover, Weeks and Tabernacles. According to the tradition, all of them are remembrance festivals, commemorating particular moments in the complex story of the exodus[45] or the so-called history of salvation.[46] Passover recalls the flight

---

44. Frye 1982; Leach and Aycock 1983: 8; Garbini 1988; Thompson 1999; Davies 1992.

45. Gottwald suggests that the understanding of exodus may be twofold: as an event or a series of events and as a process, as a complex of events, exhibiting certain recognizable features. Gottwald 1993: 273.

46. De Vaux 1965: II, 501.

from Egypt, Weeks celebrates the covenant on Sinai, while Tabernacles recollects the forty years spent wandering through the wilderness. Among them, Passover is the only one that is in the Pentateuch firmly connected to the salvation saga. Numbers mentions the exodus story in connection with Passover sacrifice,[47] while in Deuteronomy both Passover sacrifice and the Unleavened Bread[48] are related to the departure from Egypt.[49] Tabernacles' connection with exodus and the salvation history comes only from Lev. 23.42–43, which relates the booths in which people lived during this festival with the booths in which Israel dwelt after the exodus. The connection of Weeks and the covenant on Sinai comes actually from the book of Jubilees in which all of the covenants from Noah to Sinai happen on the day of Weeks.[50] In the Pentateuch, Weeks' connection to the history of salvation is through the slavery in Egypt.[51]

Among the three festivals the focus of the Yahwistic ideological interest was on Passover and it is quite clear that it was the first to suffer theological reinterpretation. While the purpose of celebrating Weeks and Tabernacles is untouched by ideological revision (they are both openly related to the agricultural season, Weeks to the end of the wheat harvest, Tabernacles generally to the end of the agricultural works related to gathering and storing food), Passover's pre-commemorative or perhaps parallel purpose and function are completely overwritten. In the Bible it appears only as a commemoration festival that celebrates a historical event.

This relatively consistent picture that the biblical texts project at an ideological level becomes very inconsistent when it comes to ascertaining its ritual components. According to the biblical traditions, in different times and in different circumstances, Passover was quite differently performed. The disparate portrayals of Passover left their mark on the theoretical discussions about its development and meaning. Advanced hypotheses show the highest possible degree of heterogeneity and include a whole range of methodological approaches. In making their conclusions about Passover's function and development, some scholars rely on purely literary criteria, some on the methods of comparative religion, while some try to implement both. On the following pages we shall try to present their major points from the perspective of the questions that are of special interest to us, that is, the questions of Passover's dual origin and its pre-commemorative function. However, given the versatility of presented conclusions and methodological approaches we shall not try to argue our

---

47. Num. 9.1; 33.3.
48. Deut. 16.1, 3, 6.
49. Only Leviticus fails to mention the exodus. Lev. 23.5–6.
50. Jub. 6.15–17; 14.18–20; 15.1–4.
51. Deut. 16.11–12.

point of view in contrast to these theories, choosing instead to deal summarily with them through discussing Passover legislative passages on which these theories rely for their support.

The majority of theories start from the assumption that the Israelites were nomads/semi-nomads/pastoralists and that the Yahwistic Passover was in fact an amalgam of two distinct festivals, one typical of the Israelites with nomadic-pastoral features and the other typical of the farming population of Palestine and their sedentary way of life and customs related to agriculture. The period of using unleavened bread is usually taken to represent the agricultural feast, while the ritual performed on its first day with the characteristic animal sacrifice is explained as a heritage from the nomadic-pastoral past of the Israelites. Which trait of this first-day ritual is taken as characteristic of the Israelites' nomadic/ pastoralist heritage and used as evidence for the previously mentioned hypothesis, is a matter that varies from author to author.

J. Wellhausen maintained that the Passover sacrifice was originally a nomadic-pastoral thanksgiving festival unrelated to any particular season. Its main feature was the sacrifice of firstlings. The Feast of the Unleavened Bread, on the other hand, was one of three Canaanite festivals that marked prominent stages in the agricultural year: Unleavened Bread and Weeks marked the beginning and the end of the corn harvest, while Tabernacles was a feast of vintage and bringing of the corn from the threshing floors. With the Deuteronomic centralization, both Passover sacrifice and Unleavened Bread lost their primary connection with nature. They were combined and in the process the Unleavened Bread was historicized as part of the exodus commemoration.[52]

According to G. Beer, Passover originally consisted of three separate springtime festivals.[53] One was a nocturnal firstling sacrifice held at full moon, which was part of the Israelite nomadic heritage. After the settlement in Canaan, it was performed only by the people of Judah. In contrast to the majority of scholars who posit that the family dwelling was the place of its observance, Beer holds that it was held in local sanctuaries as an introductory rite for the harvest season. The sacrificial animal had divine properties. It was consumed whole with unleavened bread, since leaven was regarded as ritually impure.[54] At some stage, in commemoration of the tenth plague, a smearing of blood was introduced into the original pattern. The innovation changed the place of its observance; instead of local shrines, it was now held in individual houses. However, the innovation did not acquire great importance before the exile.[55] In the

---

52. Wellhausen 1885: 83–94. Also Beer 1912: 9; May 1936: 66.
53. Beer 1912: 9.
54. Beer 1912: 23.
55. Beer 1912: 26.

time of Josiah, this firstling sacrifice achieved a status of national ceremony; its observance was limited to the central shrine in Jerusalem; the sacrificial animal did not have to be a firstling anymore;[56] the rite of blood smearing was abandoned; the ritual was no longer held as a commemoration of the tenth plague, but of the exodus. The flesh of the sacrifice was now to be boiled instead of being roasted. The people in the northern kingdom had their own version of a vernal nocturnal festival, held at the full moon. It was the Feast of the Unleavened Bread, observed before the spring harvest. According to Beer, the feast may have lasted either one or seven days. The third feast, also held in spring, was the offering of the first sheaf of barley and was held at the local shrines.[57] The merging between the southern Passover and the northern Feast of the Unleavened Bread came as a consequence of the religious reform of Ezekiel.[58]

G.B. Gray also believed that, originally, Passover sacrifice was observed by nomadic Israelites. It happened on the night of the full moon nearest the spring equinox. Its main feature was the sacrificial meal and in its earliest form consisted of eating raw flesh of the animal together with the bones and blood. For his theory he finds support in the prohibition against eating raw flesh and breaking of the bones in Exod. 12.9 and 12.46 which he held to be against actual practice.[59] The custom was later modified and the animal was cooked while its blood was smeared on the doorposts. It was an apotropaic ritual that was intended to protect the people inside the house. The centralization of the cult changed the ritual by abandoning the smearing of the blood on the door and only the sacrificial meal continued to be practised.[60]

R. de Vaux starts from the same notion as Beer and Gray that Passover sacrifice was a spring festival of nomadic shepherds.[61] He finds a parallel between Passover ritual and the sacrifices of the ancient Arabs where, similar to Passover, there is neither altar nor priests. However, he rejects the view of Wellhausen that it was a thanksgiving festival of firstlings, claiming that its main purpose was to secure fecundity and prosperity for the flock.[62] The focus of the ritual was on the use of blood which shows that it was apotropaic in nature.[63] The smearing of blood on the stiles of the door[64] suggests that it was carried out in order to drive away evil

---

56. Beer 1912: 31.
57. Beer 1912: 28.
58. Beer 1912: 33.
59. Also Smith 1907: 344–45.
60. Gray 1925: 337–82.
61. De Vaux 1965: II, 484.
62. De Vaux 1965: II, 489.
63. De Vaux 1965: II, 492.; 1978: 366. Also Ringgren 1966: 186–87; Zeitlin 1984: 86.
64. Exod. 12.7, 22.

powers, 'the destroyer', mentioned in Exod. 12.23 and Exod. 12.13.[65] On the other hand, the Feast of the Unleavened Bread was a Canaanite agricultural festival, marking the beginning of the harvest in spring.[66] In contrast to Passover which was a family festival, the Feast of the Unleavened Bread had a pilgrimage character. Both celebrations were observed in spring. Josiah's centralization also transformed Passover sacrifice into a pilgrimage festival and the obvious consequence was the amalgamation of the two feasts into a single festival.[67]

S. Mowinckel also holds that the first day of Passover was a remnant of the semi-nomadic past of the Israelites. It was a family ritual. The sacrificial animal represented the deity and those who ate of its flesh absorbed some of its divine qualities. It was expected that the deity would resurrect, which was the reason for the prohibition on breaking the bones of the sacrificial animal. In the annual recital of the Passover, Mowinckel finds a trace of a re-enactment of a cultic drama.[68] Initially, Passover was not associated with the exodus. With the promulgation of the P code, however, the exodus story became its key moment. Passover became increasingly important when it was artificially amalgamated with the Canaanite agricultural ceremony, the Festival of the Unleavened Bread.[69]

J. Pedersen finds that the emphasis on firstborn and firstlings in the Exodus narrative indicates that Passover sacrifice was originally a ritual of sanctification of the firstborn performed by the Israelite nomads.[70] In contrast to other scholars, he allows a slight possibility that eating of unleavened bread might also have been a remnant of the Israelites' bedouin past.[71] However, its seven-day use strongly indicates that it was an independent feast rather than just an amplification of a custom associated with Passover. From that perspective the Feast of the Unleavened Bread could only have been a Canaanite festival related to the barley harvest, the purpose of which was sanctification of the first produce of the soil. Its main trait was consumption of new crops without the pollution of leaven. The two festivals, Passover sacrifice and the Unleavened Bread, were both celebrated in spring and both performed essentially the same function: sanctification. These coincidences provided a common basis for their merger.[72] At some unspecified point in history they were connected to the exodus legend which resulted in the loss of their original significance. The Feast of the Unleavened Bread had nothing to do any more with new

65. Also Kaufmann 1961: 115.
66. De Vaux 1965: 490.
67. De Vaux 1965: 486.
68. Mowinckel 1922: 37.
69. Mowinckel 1922: 204–206.
70. Pedersen 1959: 398.
71. Pedersen 1959: 399.
72. Pedersen 1959: 400–401.

crops, neither did Passover sacrifice with firstborns. The combined feast became a commemorative celebration through which people re-lived the events on which their existence as an independent nation was based. Through mimetic acts, such as eating in haste, with staff in hand and with girded loins, they re-lived the legend and thereby sanctified their history.[73] With the strengthening influence of the Jerusalem temple, Passover became a pilgrimage festival. The Deuteronomic reform managed to partially transform it into a temple festival. It kept its essentially family character and in the years preceding the second destruction of the temple its celebration involved both temple and family contexts.[74]

Accepting the traditional approach, H. Ringgren also maintains that originally there were two separate festivals which were combined at an uncertain point in history. The Feast of the Unleavened Bread was rooted in the agricultural civilization and associated with the beginning of the barley harvest. The unleavened cakes represented the first produce of the land and were eaten in order to release the new harvest for profane use. Passover sacrifice, on the other hand, probably originated among the nomadic Israelites. It was observed in spring, at the time of transhumance in order to protect the herds and promote the fertility of animals. The purpose of the prohibition of breaking the bones of the sacrifice may have been to assure the continuing life of the animal.[75]

G. Fohrer also claims that before the settlement of the Israelites in Canaan, Passover sacrifice was a nomadic ritual, probably performed immediately before the spring migrations.[76] After the settlement, it ceased to be celebrated, since it lost every meaning in the context of settled life. It was revived by the Deuteronomic law when it was associated with the Feast of the Unleavened Bread and provided with a historical basis.[77] The Unleavened Bread was one of the pilgrimage Canaanite festivals. It was an agricultural feast, held at the beginning of the barley harvest. The date of its observance was not fixed, since it depended on the ripening of the grain. Its main characteristic was the eating of new grain without leaven, that is, without any addition from the old harvest. It lasted for seven days. Israelites incorporated this festival into Yahwism by referring it to Yahweh and connecting it with the flight from Egypt.[78]

For H.J. Kraus, Passover sacrifice was originally a nomadic rite performed by the clan or camp community. It was observed in spring before the seasonal migration in order to protect animals and people

73. Pedersen 1959: 401–409.
74. Pedersen 1959: 412–15.
75. Ringgren 1966: 186.
76. Fohrer 1973: 40.
77. Fohrer 1973: 100–101.
78. Fohrer 1973: 202.

against demons and attacks of hostile tribes. The transition from desert to cultivated land took place on a fixed date, probably on the night of the full moon in spring. After the settlement, the annual movement from the desert was looked upon in the light of historical traditions and connected with the flight from Egypt.[79] In the time of the Judges, it was still a communal feast, connected with Gilgal, the cultic centre of the tribal confederation.[80] This archaic pattern dissolved in the time of the monarchy, when Passover became a family festival celebrated in villages. Its pilgrimage character was revived with Josiah's religious reform.[81] Following Wellhausen, Kraus maintains that Unleavened Bread was a Canaanite thanksgiving festival, celebrated after the spring equinox which lasted seven days. Israelites adopted it, but in a modified and reshaped version. The celebration was directed towards Yahweh instead of Baal, who was the original deity. The referral to Yahweh excluded the nature myth and removed laments about the dying god of vegetation. The festival was centralized and also historicized.[82]

M. Haran claims that the 'dramatic embellishments' of Passover sacrifice such as collective participation in the ritual, choosing the animal from the flocks rather than the herds, hurried eating of roasted meat at night in a dramatic atmosphere and the emphasis on blood, demonstrate its nomadic origin. The Unleavened Bread was an agricultural festival of the barley harvest. It marked the beginning of the harvest season and was connected to the Weeks festival which marked its end when the wheat harvest was over. It was a temple festival and the worshippers had to make a pilgrimage to one of the city temples. Initially, only the males were obliged to attend it, but in time whole families took part in it.[83] Haran disputes the idea that centralization was responsible for linking Passover sacrifice and the Feast of the Unleavened Bread given that all the sources recognize them as already connected. The amalgamation happened at an early stage of the Israelites' history and from the sources it is not possible to assume when.[84] He also disputes that the merger happened because of the intrinsic similarities between the functions of the two festivals and regards it as a matter of circumstances. The Unleavened Bread had its

79. Kraus 1966: 46–47.

80. In a similar vein, Cross suggests that Passover was the spring festival of the tribal league at Gilgal and that it was marked by the reciting and enactment of the exodus and conquest traditions. Its main function was the renewal of the covenant that made the basis of the community's common life. Cross 1973: 84–86.

81. Kraus 1966: 162–63.

82. Kraus 1966: 48–49.

83. Haran 1985: 289–96.

84. Haran 1985: 342.

place only in a settled life, while Passover sacrifice was connected only to the nomadic conditions.[85]

Acknowledging that a purely nomadic past of the Israelites is an untenable assumption, R. Albertz attempts to interpret the Passover in Exodus as a pastoral rite that could reflect some of the rhythm of life in transhumance conditions. He accepts the interpretation that Passover sacrifice was a religious accompaniment to the change from winter to summer pastures claiming that features such as its spring date, the hurried eating, the prohibition against leaving anything of the sacrificial animal and the performance of the blood rite to avert the destroyer point to the context of transhumance life.[86] However, the main religious focus of the peasant population were the three great annual festivals which followed the agricultural cycle of production, the Feast of the Unleavened Bread at the beginning of the grain harvest, Weeks at the end of the wheat harvest and Tabernacles after the fruit and grapes harvest. In Albertz's view the cycle of festivals goes back to pre-monarchic times. When the Exodus group entered Palestine, Yahweh simply took his place in an already existing festival cult. The purpose of these feasts was to secure the blessing for the land and to express gratitude for the produce. In time, they were successively historicized by taking on the function of commemorating the history of the foundation of Israel.[87] The Deuteronomic reform movement changed the traditional family Passover into a pilgrimage festival and combined it with the Unleavened Bread.[88] During the exile a reverse development took place. Because it was not possible anymore to celebrate the combined feast of the Deuteronomic reform centrally, in a temple, Passover reverted to its old family form that could be observed in individual homes. The father of the family again became responsible for its organization. The main concern of this decentralized Passover focused on the participants who were to be allowed to take part in its celebration and on fixing a single date. In the specific circumstances of the exile the Feast of the Unleavened Bread lost its harvest significance and was simply attached to Passover.[89]

B.M. Levinson also believes that Passover sacrifice and the Unleavened Bread were originally separate occasions. In contrast to the Unleavened Bread, Passover sacrifice did not have the character of a festival and the worshippers were not obliged to undertake the pilgrimage to one of the local sanctuaries to pay homage to the deity. Prior to the Deuteronomic reform, the slaughter of the sacrificial animal was a ritual performed

85. Haran 1985: 320–21.
86. Albertz 1994: 35.
87. Albertz 1994: 89–90.
88. Albertz 1994: 208.
89. Albertz 1994: 410–11.

entirely within the context of the clan. The emphasis on the clan and the limited choice of sacrificial animals to those coming from flocks stem from the nomadic Israelite culture of the pre-settlement period. Originally, Passover sacrifice was a ritualized slaughter with an apotropaic function which is, according to Levinson, evident from the use of the blood. The act of smearing and the use of hyssop also attest to its protective purpose against destructive agents. Marking of the doorway with blood constitutes the establishment of a liminal zone between the interior of the house as a refuge and the exterior as the realm of uncontrolled destructive powers. The protective effect is achieved through sympathetic magic. The lamb's blood on the door is regarded as a substitute for the blood of the house's occupants.[90] According to Levinson, the pre-Deuteronomistic Passover sacrifice was in contradiction to the norms of the Israelite sacrificial practice in several aspects: specification of the animal (chosen only from the flocks while the normative sacrifice included both herds and flocks); location of the slaughter (doorway rather than altar); disposition of the blood (daubing of the doorway rather than being thrown against the altar); and the method of cooking (roasting rather than boiling). The Deuteronomic reform which amalgamated Passover sacrifice and the Feast of the Unleavened Bread crucially changed the manner of their observance. With the centralization, Passover became a pilgrimage festival while its sacrificial component was brought into line with other temple sacrifices. The apotropaic blood ritual was abandoned, it was permitted for the slaughtered animal to also come from the herds, its preparation was changed from roasting to cooking and, above all, Passover lost its domestic, local context. The pre-Deuteronomistic Festival of the Unleavened Bread was one of the three annual festivals (Unleavened Bread, Harvest and Ingathering) that required the male Israelites to make a pilgrimage to the local temple. Its main feature was the removal of anything leaven and eating unleavened bread for a period of seven days. The seventh day was the culmination marked by a journey to the local sanctuary where a sacrifice was offered.[91] With the centralization of the cult to the Jerusalem temple, the Feast of the Unleavened Bread suffered opposite changes to those of Passover. It lost its status of a pilgrimage since it was no longer connected to the altar and was marked only by eating the unleavened bread for a seven-day period.[92]

In contrast to many scholars, I. Engnell and J.B. Segal maintain that Passover was never a combination of two feasts that originated from different cultural backgrounds.[93] Engnell rejects the claims that Passover

---

90. Levinson 1997: 57–60.
91. Levinson 1997: 66–68.
92. Levinson 1997: 79–80.
93. Engnell 1952; Segal 1963.

sacrifice was a firstling sacrifice with an apotropaic function. He also rejects the idea that the ritual had a family character. Instead, he finds in it remnants of much better-known festivals from Mesopotamia and Canaan, which followed the cycle of nature. According to him, Passover sacrifice was the Israelite festival *par excellence*. He connects the name 'pesah' with the terms 'limp' or 'dance' as in a cultic dance. The sacrificial animal was a substitution sacrifice and the sacrificers mourned while they danced. Engnell also finds remains of a sham fight in the story of the defeat of the Pharaoh. The ritual drama culminated in a nocturnal celebration with a victory hymn preserved in Exod. 15.1–12. According to Engnell, the judgments against the Pharaoh are reminiscent of the judgment theme of the Babylonian Akitu festival. The resurrection theme in Passover was also preserved through the prayers for dew at the modern Jewish Passover, while the theme of the sacred marriage is still reflected in the Song of Songs which is in modern times recited on the eighth day of the festival. Engnell also points to the ritual similarities that exist between Passover and the Babylonian Akitu. Both were celebrated in spring, in the month of Nisan. Both lasted for eleven days if Passover is reckoned from the first day of preparation on the 10th of Nisan. During the Akitu there was a re-enactment of the victory over Tiamat, the primeval sea, and her consort Kingu. In Passover we have the parallel in Sea of Reeds and the Pharaoh. Finally, the wilderness wanderings are reminiscent of the Babylonian Akitu, a portion of which was celebrated in the open country. Engnell, nevertheless, maintains that originally there were two festivals that were combined. The difference between them was the region from which they originated. Passover was the southern variant of the Canaanite vernal New Year festival and, due to the conditions in that part of Palestine, its accent was on animals. In the north, the accent of the New Year festival was on the produce of the land, hence the unleavened bread. The fusion between the northern and the southern festival happened not because they were both celebrated in spring, but because of their fundamentally same character. In both, the focus was on maintaining fertility and on re-establishing the cosmos. In the course of time, the combined festival was historicized; it lost its dramatic character and became a family feast dominated by the component of the unleavened bread.[94]

The most exhaustive analysis of Passover was done by Segal. Similar to Engnell, his leading idea is that Passover was a vernal New Year festival dedicated to the national god, which from the earliest times was celebrated on a fixed date, the date of the spring equinox. It was a pilgrimage festival and was celebrated in a central shrine.[95] In addition to fulfilling religious

94.   Engnell 1952: 39–50.
95.   Segal 1963: 114.

obligations, the celebration was also an occasion for a census when male adults were numbered for military purposes.[96] Ritual purity was required of both the sacrificial animals and the participants since the ritual was to be held at a sacred place. The festival lasted for seven-days, which shows that it was a rite of passage, given the fact that a seven day period is characteristic of all the Israelite rites of passage. It was probably also preceded by a seven-day pre-liminal period of purification.[97] As a New Year festival, it was presumably marked by a sacred procession, as was the case in other Near Eastern civilizations. However, while in other similar festivals the procession culminated in an exodus from the cultivated regions into the desert as a reflection of seasonal changes or in search of the vegetation deity, that rite in Passover has been preserved solely through the story of the exodus.[98] In other cultures, the seasons in which New Year festivals were celebrated were the seasons of fixing the destinies for the oncoming year, deciding on who will live and who will die. Therefore, the Passover sacrifice and the smearing of the blood had a redemptive purpose, rather than apotropaic.[99] Eating of the flesh of the sacrificial animal by the family was an act of communion between the family members, while the blood on the doorposts of the house was a sign that the whole family was to be redeemed. The meal was accompanied by the eating of unleavened bread, leaven being avoided for reasons of ritual purity. Ritual purity is also in the background of the regulation against the breaking of the bones of the sacrifice.[100]

According to Segal, Passover and Unleavened Bread were never two separate feasts which fused into a single one. In his opinion, quite the contrary is true. In the Bible narrative, they were divided into two celebrations, 'because only one group of ceremonies, the Pesah, appeared to have the full relevance to the circumstances of the Exodus'.[101] The use of unleavened bread was in fact Passover's distinctive feature. However, its consumption was not associated with the harvest, but rather with avoidance of impurity. Unlike the majority of scholars who claim that Passover marked the beginning of the harvest, Segal claims that Passover was actually observed before the harvest and that essentially it did not have anything to do with the harvest. The month of Abib, the month of Passover, was the month when the corn was still green and not suitable for

96.   Segal 1963: 137.
97.   Segal 1963: 138.
98.   Segal 1963: 151.
99.   Segal 1963: 163.
100. Segal 1963: 171.
101. Segal uses the term 'Pesah' to denote the sacrifice during the first night of the festival. Segal 1963: 175.

harvesting. A real harvest thanksgiving festival was the feast of Weeks, celebrated seven weeks after the sheaf-offering.[102]

T. Gaster views Passover as a festival that originally consisted of a nocturnal meal during which the sacrificial victim was consumed roasted and with unleavened bread. The eating of the unleavened bread continued for the next seven days so that the entire celebration became known as the Feast of the Unleavened Bread. The original purpose of the meal was 'to re-cement ties of kinship, infuse new life into the family, and renew the bonds of mutual protection at the beginning of each year'.[103] The common life was renewed through eating of the flesh of the sacrificial victim and bread, and special precautions were undertaken to avoid any contamination of these two mediating agents. Therefore the meat was eaten in a hurry before it became putrescent and for the same reason whatever was not consumed had to be burnt the following morning. The bread was unleavened because leavened food is fermented and fermentation implies putrescence. The family reunion meal also meant restoration of the alliance with the family god thus ensuring his protection during the coming year. The outward manifestation of this kinship alliance between human and divine members was represented by a sign made in blood since the idea of kinship implies shared blood. The blood was that of the sacrificial animal. Gaster points out that rituals can have more than one meaning and that, in the case of Passover, the festival had an apotropaic function to avert evil and misfortune that may befall the people, the stock and the fields.[104]

J. Van Seters also disputes the notion that Passover sacrifice and Unleavened Bread were separate festivals. However, in contrast to other scholars, he argues that Unleavened Bread was not an agricultural feast of the Canaanites, but rather an innovation of the exilic period when it was not possible to properly observe Passover sacrifice because the temple was destroyed. Eating of the unleavened bread became a basis of a substitute festival. Before the introduction of unleavened bread consumption, Passover was a one-day spring feast held at the local sanctuary. An animal from the flock was killed and eaten with unleavened bread. Deuteronomy restricted its observance to the central sanctuary and transformed it into a commemoration festival celebrating exodus. During the exile the only feature that was kept was the eating of the unleavened bread. After the return from the exile, Passover was revived in the restored temple. However, further modifications occurred because its temple observance presented a problem for the Jews in diaspora. To accommodate the conditions of the Jews in diaspora and in order to sanctify each

102.   Segal 1963: 179.
103.   Gaster 1958: 18.
104.   Gaster 1958: 13–25.

household, the blood rite – the smearing of the blood on the doors – was introduced, while the sacrificial animals were prepared in such a way as to resemble an offering by fire.[105]

In contrast to all previously mentioned scholars who maintain that Passover was not originally connected with the exodus, T.D. Alexander claims that the assumption that the latter sources created an historical aetiology for the ritual is not supported by evidence and that in all Pentateuch sources the two are already firmly linked. According to him it has to be accepted that the explanation for the term 'pesah' given in Exodus 12–13 is still the most suitable.[106] Starting from this perspective he views the passages in Exodus 12–13 as both a description of the first Passover in Egypt as well as instructions for future observances. The first Passover, given the historical circumstances, was different from the model that would be practiced only in subsequent years. The particular situation explains its uniqueness. The animal was killed by the elders[107] and not by priests because the Aaronic priesthood was not as yet established. For the same reason no meat was put aside for priestly consumption and there is no reference to a central sanctuary or an altar which were instituted only after the exodus. The animal was killed either near or in the houses. Alexander believes that the historical context also explains why Passover sacrifice took place at twilight in contrast to other sacrifices that were offered during the day. In his view, being used as a workforce by the Egyptians, the Israelites did not have much opportunity to offer sacrifices during daytime. He also claims that the timing of Passover, the night of the full moon, was the most opportune time for the preparations given the impending departure of the Israelites from Egypt. He finds that this first Passover (killing of the animal, eating the meat with unleavened bread and burning of the remains the following morning) parallels the ritual for consecrating the Aaronic priests. This leads him to conclude that the purpose of Passover was consecration by which the Israelites set themselves apart as holy. Later Passover observances were performed in a temple through a week-long Festival of Unleavened Bread with special commemoration of the Passover night.[108]

It should be noted that the origin of the festival has been also sought in the etymology of the word 'pesah'. The word has been connected with a Hebrew verb *psh* meaning 'protect, save'[109] or 'limp, dance with limping motions',[110] as well as with some words from cognate Semitic languages,

105. Van Seters 1983: 169–81.
106. Alexander 1995: 5–6.
107. Exod. 12.21.
108. Alexander 1995: 6–11.
109. Isa. 31.5.
110. 1 Kgs 18.26.

such as the Accadian *passahu* ('make soft, supple, soothe, placate'), Egyptian words meaning 'harvest', 'commemoration' or 'blow', and Arabic *fsh* ('separate').[111]

It is evident from the above review that with respect to the origins and development of Passover, either as a whole or any of its individual features, there is hardly any consensus among scholars. It seems that the only points of convergence are its annual character, spring as the season in which it was performed and its antiquity, although even for them there are opposing positions.[112] With recent developments in the theory of early Israelite history at least some of the proposed views can be eliminated as inconsistent with the wider picture. That is most certainly true in the case of the claim that Passover sacrifice was of nomadic origin and as such typical of the Israelites, while the Unleavened Bread was characteristic of the sedentary Canaanites and their agrarian religious customs. Today, we can be almost sure that both of them were of sedentary and Canaanite origin. That knowledge, however, although extremely important in terms of providing a definite cultural context and a clear direction for our investigation of Passover, does not resolve the primary question that we are interested in: whether it was a single festival from the beginning or whether it was an amalgam of two separate units. It might seem that knowing the Israelites belonged to the same cultural and ethnic stock as the rest of Palestine's population gives us a good reason to discard the idea that there were originally two feasts and to accordingly treat the ritual as a single unit. However, we cannot rule out the possibility that, although both of Canaanite origin, there were indeed two feasts that came from different segments of the Canaanite society, from the pastoral and the agricultural,[113] and that at some stage they were merged in a single festival. There is also the possibility that even if both originated from the same cultural and economic background, they were different in character, that Passover sacrifice was a family ritual, while Unleavened Bread was a temple festival. The knowledge about the origins of Israelites also does not resolve the problem of Passover's pre-commemorative function to which the presented theories offer very insightful answers which cannot be discarded solely on account of their false initial premise. However, in the light of the current understanding of the early Israelites' history and their origins it is clear that Engnell's and Segal's views, which attempt to find unifying ideas behind the diversity of biblical presentations of Passover, are of greatest significance for the purposes of this work.

111. Segal 1963: 95–97; Sarna 1986: 86–87.
112. Wellhausen, for example, thought that Passover sacrifice was not connected to any particular season (1885: 83), while Van Seters believes that the Unleavened Bread was an innovation of the exile (1983: 169–81).
113. Lemche 1988: 219. Also Albertz 1994: 35.

PART II

Chapter 2

DEVELOPMENT OF PASSOVER

2.1. *The Question of Centralization*

The majority of scholars that advance the hypothesis that Passover was a combination of two originally independent feasts believes that the amalgamation was a consequence of the centralization,[1] a trend in the cultic practice to restrict the place of legal sacrificial worship to a single sanctuary. It is commonly held that such a trend is reflected in the book of Deuteronomy and that the Deuteronomic laws on Passover bear witness of the fusion. Based on the account in 2 Kings 23, it is also very often assumed that the first attempt to centralize the cult and consequently Passover was carried out by the Judahite king Josiah in the seventh century BCE.[2]

Whether anything like the dramatic events described in the Bible[3] ever took place during Josiah or whether the story is historically a much later attempt by Jerusalem's priests to legitimize the authority of their temple is a question that is open to debate. What is certain, however, is that in post-exilic times the real centralization of the cult manifested not as a sudden reform, but as a strenuous and long historical process. Its main aim was to elevate the Jerusalem temple to the status of being the single place where sacrificial worship could legally be performed. In terms of that objective the centralization never fully materialized. Although becoming the most reputable, the Jerusalem temple never became the only temple where Yahweh was worshipped. Even as late as the Hasmonean period, there was the temple in Leontopolis, while the Samaritans, even after John Hircanus destroyed their sanctuary, stubbornly refused to recognize the authority of Jerusalem and continued to regard Mount Gerizim as Yahweh's chosen place.

---

1. Wellhausen 1885: 88; De Vaux 1965: II, 485; Nicolsky 1927: 171–241; Fohrer 1973: 100–101; Kraus 1966: 49–50; Albertz 1994: 208; Levinson 1997; Nakanose 1993: 8.

2. Some, though, hold that it is not possible to determine the period in which the fusion took place because the amalgamation happened naturally over time and the written sources only sanctioned what was already a practice. Ringgren 1966: 186; Haran 1985: 342; Pedersen 1959: 401–409.

3. 2 Kgs 22–23; 2 Chron. 34–35.

The controversy between the Jerusalemites and the Samaritans regarding the temple that will be the only legitimate place of sacrificial worship perhaps derives from the book of Deuteronomy, which although insists on a single sanctuary[4] never actually gives the precise location of the place to which the sacrificial worship is to be restricted. Most of the time it refers to it as the place which the Lord will choose for his name to dwell in. As much as scholars habitually connect this chosen place with Jerusalem, the point is that it could equally refer to Mount Gerizim or for that matter any other location as long as the temple is in the promized land and dedicated to Yahweh. Deuteronomy is a programmatic book and its laws are orientated towards the future of Israel. The central temple is part of that idealized future and as such a projection that is yet to find its realization. From this perspective it is possible to claim that in historical terms Deuteronomy preceded the centralization. On the other hand, it is equally possible to claim that rather than being a base on which the squabbles between the Jews and the Samaritans were built, its omission to name the central temple is a reflection of the reality and is intended as a diplomatic ploy to give legitimacy to both Jerusalem and Gerizim. For us, however, the question of the historical period in which Deuteronomic legislation was formed is not of any interest. What is important is that in terms of binding the cultic practice to a single place there is a significant correspondence between the reality of the centralization and the requirements of Deuteronomy. This fact significantly improves the credibility of this biblical book as a source of information. In times immediately before the destruction of the second temple, the sacrificial worship, including the observance of the three main festivals, was mainly performed at Yahweh's chosen place, as stipulated in Deuteronomy.

While the effects of centralization on Weeks and Tabernacles hardly ever attract scholarly attention, apart from acknowledging that they were to be performed in the central sanctuary, Passover is assumed to have been greatly affected by them, both structurally and functionally. The basic line of reasoning is that the observance of Passover sacrifice, originally a family rite performed in the family dwellings, was transferred to the central temple thereby changing its character into a pilgrimage temple feast. The transformation led to its fusion with the Unleavened Bread, the original pilgrimage festival. This explanation is mainly based on the assumed difference in presenting Passover in the Exodus sources and comparisons between their descriptions and that of Deuteronomy. The presumably older E and J sources, which designate Unleavened Bread[5] as a pilgrimage feast without explicitly mentioning Passover sacrifice, are taken as evidence that the latter did not have the character of

4. Deut. 12.13.
5. Exod. 23.15; 34.18.

a pilgrimage before the centralization, given that Deuteronomy explicitly demands it to be performed at the temple on the first day of the Feast of the Unleavened Bread.[6] However, when the presumption that E and J from Exodus are older than D is removed, the basic picture of Passover emerging from those sources is in complete concordance with Deuteronomy. It is a pilgrimage festival[7] that lasts seven days[8] and is marked by two distinctive traits, the killing of Passover animals (pesah)[9] and avoidance of leaven[10] for the whole duration of the festival that is ritually translated as the eating of unleavened bread.[11] From this perspective, the names Passover sacrifice (pesah) and Unleavened Bread appear to be synonymous.

R. de Vaux, one of many who sees Passover as a combination of two originally independent feasts, believes that the artificiality of their connection is preserved and still detectable in the Deuteronomic legislation itself.[12] According to him, there is an apparent contradiction between 16.1, 2, 4b-7, which he assigns to Passover sacrifice and 16.3, 4a, and 8 which he connects with the Feast of the Unleavened Bread.[13] He argues that if the people were to go home on the first morning after the sacrifice was offered in the temple, as 16.7 indicates, they could not stay to eat the unleavened bread in the temple on the seventh day, as he interprets the stipulation in 16.8.

It has to be noted, though, that de Vaux's reading and interpretation of the verses comes from an already predetermined point of view which differentiates between Passover sacrifice and Unleavened Bread as

6.   Deut. 16.1–8, 16.
7.   Exod. 23.14–15; 34.18.
8.   Exod. 13.6; 23.15.
9.   Exod. 12.21, 27; 34.25.
10.   Exod. 13.7.
11.   Exod. 13.3, 6, 7.
12.   De Vaux 1965: II, 485–86.
13.   Deut. 16. (1) Observe the month of Abib, and keep the passover to the Lord your God; for in the month of Abib the Lord your God brought you out of Egypt by night. (2) And you shall offer the passover sacrifice to the Lord your God, from the flock or the herd, at the place which the Lord will choose, to make his name dwell there. (3) You shall eat no leavened bread with it; seven days you shall eat it with unleavened bread, the bread of affliction – for you came out of the land of Egypt in hurried flight – that all days of your life you may remember the day when you came out of Egypt. (4) No leaven shall be seen with you in all your territory for seven days; nor shall any of the flesh which you sacrifice on the evening of the first day remain all night until morning. (5) You may not offer the passover sacrifice within any of your towns which the Lord your God gives you; (6) but at the place which the Lord your God will choose, to make his name dwell in it, there you shall offer the passover sacrifice, in the evening at the going of the sun, at the time you came out of Egypt. (7) And you shall boil it and eat it at the place which the Lord will choose; and in the morning you shall turn and go to your tents. For six days you shall eat unleavened bread; and on the seventh day there shall be solemn assembly to the Lord your God; you shall do no work on it.

independent feasts. So, if eating of unleavened bread is mentioned, as in 16.8, it is immediately seen as part of the festival of Unleavened Bread which in turn results in all other kinds of presumptions, such as its pilgrimage character, temple bound performance, and so on. However, an open-minded and more attentive reader will notice that in 16.8 it is not categorically stated that the meeting on the seventh day should take place in the central temple. It is merely declared that the 'solemn assembly' will happen, but without further directions regarding the place of the gathering. This failure to mandate the central temple as the location for the assembly can hardly be accidental, given that centralized worship is one of the most significant and most distinctive ideas of Deuteronomic ideology. It is quite unlikely that the author would have missed yet one more opportunity to use his favourite phrase, 'the place which Lord will choose for his name to dwell in', in order to emphasize the pre-eminence of the central temple for the purposes of cultic worship, including religious gathering as was the solemn assembly on the seventh day of Passover. In the legislation for Tabernacles, for example, it is unambiguously stated that all the seven days of the feast will be held 'at the place which the Lord will choose'.[14]

The silence of Deuteronomy regarding the place of the assembly on the seventh day leaves open the possibility that, apart from the central temple, it was to be held in other places as well. 'A solemn assembly', as can be learnt from other biblical texts, usually means a religious gathering in the temple of the god for whom the meeting is called for. In 2 Kgs 10.20–21 Jehu proclaims a solemn assembly for Baal, which is subsequently held in Baal's temple. In Joel 1.14 the prophet calls for a solemn assembly to be kept at Yahweh's temple, the house of the Lord. However, given that Deuteronomy permits cultic worship only in one place, that is in a single sanctuary,[15] but is in the case of the assembly on the seventh day of Passover silent regarding its location, it is most likely that for those not living in the nearest vicinity of the temple the gathering was to be held in the places where they lived and worked, around local altars, or perhaps on the communal threshing floors which seem to have served as meeting places for a variety of purposes and had some kind of sanctity attributed to them. In Exod. 50.10 Joseph performs the mourning rites for his father on the threshing floor of Atad. Gideon's test of Yahweh in Judg. 6.36–39 also takes place on a threshing floor. Uzzah gets struck by Yahweh on the

14.   Deut. 16.15: For seven days you shall keep the feast to the Lord your God at the place which the Lord will choose; because the Lord your God will bless you in all the work of your produce and in all the work of your hands, so that you will be altogether joyful.

15.   Deut. 12.13–14: (13) Take heed that you do not offer your burnt offerings at every place that you see; (14) but at the place which the Lord will choose in one of your tribes, there you shall offer your burnt offerings, and there you shall do all that I am commanding you.

threshing floor of Nacon.[16] In 2 Sam. 24.18–26 David builds an altar to Yahweh on the threshing floor. In 1 Kgs 21.10 prophets prophesy on the threshing floor. Finally, Solomon builds the Jerusalem temple on a site of a threshing floor.[17]

Wherever the gathering on the seventh day of Passover might have taken place, the indirect permission of the Deuteronomist to have it away from the 'place which the Lord will choose for his name to dwell in' means that he did not have the intention to centralize the feast for a full seven days of its duration, but rather only its first day. That this is the case is evident also from the special attention he pays to the place of observing the opening ritual of the festival, that is the Passover sacrifice. The sanctioning and restricting the performance of this ritual to the central temple is reiterated no less than three times. The first time it is merely stated that it should be offered at the 'place which the Lord will choose for his name to dwell in'.[18] The second time the establishment of the exclusive relationship between the central temple and the opening ritual follows the ban on its performance in any of the towns.[19] Finally, Yahweh's place is mentioned in connection with the preparation and eating of the flesh of the sacrificed animal.[20] In contrast to Passover sacrifice, the eating of the unleavened bread, the other distinct ritual of the festival that lasted for seven days, is never mentioned in connection with the chosen place. The intention behind Passover legislation in Deuteronomy is obviously not the centralization of the whole festival, but only of the rituals and ceremonies on its first day. For ordinary people, the days following the offering and eating of the Passover sacrifice and until the seventh day when the second assembly takes place are in no particular way marked except by consumption of the unleavened bread as its ritual element and in that manner could have been observed while travelling back home or working in the fields.

The main question in this context is why would Deuteronomy, which is so characteristic in its insistence on worship in a central sanctuary, permit in the case of Passover a public religious gathering, away from it. To understand the perspective from which this seemingly divergent piece of legislation arises from the otherwise very clear centralizing trend of Deuteronomy, one needs to look at other distinctive features of this particular biblical book.

There are two widely recognized features of Deuteronomy. One is the ideological message regarding the three great unities, one people, one god,

16. 2 Sam. 6.6–8.
17. 2 Chron. 3.1.
18. Deut. 16.2.
19. Deut. 16.6.
20. Deut. 16.7.

one temple. The other one is its moral and humanistic character. Its laws are most often interpreted within the framework of these two aspects.[21] However, Deuteronomy possesses another quality that also sets it apart from other Pentateuch books, but which is hardly ever noticed. This is the Deuteronomist's sense for the practical, for the problems of everyday living, which at times proves to be extremely perceptive. In forbidding the cutting of fruit-bearing trees during a long siege he gives a very common-sense explanation as to why they should not be used for building siege works.[22] Deuteronomy also offers a practical solution to problems that can arise with the transportation of the tithe, given that it demands their deposition in the central temple. The tithe is to be turned into money and in that form taken 'to the place which the Lord your God chooses' and there spent on whatever the person desires.[23] From this last example it is obvious that Deuteronomy does not give up on what it regards as the temple's right, but that it is also keenly aware that very worldly reasons might prevent people from fulfilling religious obligations according to the centralized rules. The same concern for complications that the institution of not only central, but also sole temple, inherently generates and the subsequent attempts by Deuteronomy to somehow rectify or compensate for the consequences can be detected in its treatment of the Levites. Deuteronomy is the only book that almost invariably mentions the Levites in conjunction with the poorest among the population, 'the sojourner, the fatherless and the widow'[24] and repeatedly reminds the people not to forget them,[25] which only demonstrates that the author is aware that the centralization he advocates could bring hardship to people whose livelihood originates from sacrifices presented in temples that are now to be abandoned. If Deuteronomy's intended reform of having only one sanctuary were ever to come to fruition, the Levites who are the hereditary temple workers and who do not possess any arable land[26] might be left without any means to feed themselves. That is the reason why Deuteronomy warns the Israelites not to forget them. It even attempts to compensate for the loss of what we would call today

21.   Weinfeld 1972; Carmichael 1974; McConville 1984; Levinson 1997.

22.   Deut. 20. (19) When you besiege a city for a long time, making war against it in order to take it, you shall not destroy its trees by wielding an axe against them; for you may eat of them, but you shall not cut them down. Are the trees in the field men that they should be besieged by you? (20) Only the trees which you know are not trees for food you may destroy and cut down that you may build siegeworks against the city that makes war with you, until it fails.

23.   Deut. 14.24–26.

24.   Deut. 14.29; 16.11, 14; 26.12–13.

25.   Deut. 12.19; 14.27.

26.   Deut. 14.27: And you shall not forsake the Levite who is within your towns, for he has no portion or inheritance.

'professional achievement' by giving them the right to officiate in the central temple when they occasionally venture there and in instances they show the wish to do that.[27]

The particular spatial organization of Passover's first and last day is also a result of Deuteronomy's effort to minimize the practical shortfalls of the centralization. To restrict only the first day of the festival to the central temple while permitting its closure to be observed locally, the Deuteronomist had very good reasons related to agriculture, the main occupation of the Israelites. The observance of Passover coincided with the beginning of the season of harvesting. According to Philo at the time of the Feast of the Unleavened Bread 'the fruit of the corn has not yet reached its perfection, for the fields are in the ear stage and not yet mature for harvest...though it was to reach its perfection very shortly...'[28] Whether the barley, the first grain to be harvested in Palestine, was already ripe or not when actual celebrations of Passover took place, is not a question of any importance since its ripening most probably varied slightly each year.[29] What we can safely assume, however, is that it was certainly very close to the stage of being ready to be harvested. At such time, a request to spend a couple of days on a journey in order to stay and celebrate for a whole week in a place that is far from the standing barley, is from a farmer's perspective absurd and furthermore outright hazardous. Around the time of the harvest his most dangerous enemy is the weather. Sudden storms and hail can ruin the entire crop in a matter of hours and in such situations it is very important to be close to the fields. By permitting the last day to be celebrated locally, Deuteronomy demonstrates that it is not completely insensitive to the potentially serious implications that a prolonged pilgrimage festival at this particular time of the year might have on the outcome of the harvest and ultimately on people's lives. The big question is whether the people would have come at all to Yahweh's chosen place if at the same time that meant endangering their food supplies for the oncoming year.

The practical aspect of the Deuteronomic legislation is also manifest in the structure of Passover's working and non-working days, that is, the sanctified and non-sanctified days. Although only the last of the seven days is explicitly designated as non-working,[30] we can assume that the same is true of the first day because the people are to be in the temple

27. Deut. 18.6–7.
28. Philo, *Spec. Leg.* II, 158.
29. Trying to prove that Passover and Unleavened Bread did not have any connection with the harvest, J.H. Tigay claims that it took place before the actual harvest, but later contradicts himself when he explains that the last day of the Feast of the Unleavened Bread is to be celebrated locally because it is 'the only one that might take place during the height of the harvest...' (Tigay 1996: 152, 156).
30. Deut. 16.8.

attending and participating in the opening ceremonies and rituals.[31] The intermediary days, at least for common people, are not sanctified in any other way except by the use of unleavened bread; in every other aspect they are just ordinary days which is a provision that allows the people to get back to their homes in time for the harvest.

Passover took place during a very critical and busy season in the agricultural calendar, which by its very nature did not allow for prolonged resting or merrymaking, and Deuteronomy, although indirectly, recognizes that. The season when Tabernacles happened, for example, when both the corn and the fruit harvests were over, had an entirely different atmosphere and rhythm which the festival's legislation reflects. People are called to rejoice before Yahweh in his temple for a whole week.[32] And it was only normal that the people could indulge in feasting for such a long period because all the critical works on which depended the survival of the community until the next harvest would have been already completed. How busy was this time between Passover and Tabernacles is perhaps also indicated by the duration of the third major pilgrimage feast, Weeks, which, although equally joyful as Tabernacles, lasted for only one day and was observed after the harvest of the wheat, the last grain to ripen, was completed,[33] but before it was threshed and safely stored and before the grapes and the olives were pressed.

There is no internal inconsistency in Deuteronomic legislation on Passover that would support the much favoured hypothesis that centralization combined two separate festivals. If there is any, then it is between the book's general focus on having only one temple as a legal place of worship and the attempt to somehow compensate for the practical shortcomings of such an arrangement with respect to the particularities of the agricultural season in which Passover was observed.

As we have seen, the law in Deuteronomy centralizes only the first day of Passover to the central temple. If we posit the opposite hypothesis about Passover's origin from the usual one, namely, that it is not a combination of two originally independent feasts, the request to observe only the first day in the central temple points to a quite different direction of the festival's development from what is usually assumed. It is an indication that the centralization 'splintered' the festival because of the division forced upon its spatial organization. The division would explain the duality of its designation and the Bible's indistinct and alternative use of both Passover sacrifice and Unleavened Bread as its names.

As the discussion of J. Pierce on the Holy Week and Easter demonstrates, sometimes the unified character of a festival does not

---

31. Deut. 16.5–7.
32. Deut. 16.13–15.
33. Deut. 16.10–11.

survive because of liturgical stretching and the previously single celebration breaks down into a sequence of relatively independent feasts, each
commemorating some individual occasion in the event that is a subject of
the festival.[34] *Mutatis mutandis*, the same could be said about Passover.
The centralizing trends in the development of the cultic worship spatially
'stretched' the festival, eventually causing its collapse into two relatively
independent feasts. So, the first day that necessitated a journey to the
central temple and participation in its rituals emerged as Passover sacrifice
(pesah) while the rest of the festive days marked only by eating unleavened
bread and observed away from the temple appeared as the Feast of the
Unleavened Bread.

Such development supports the reasoning that before the spatial tension
broke down the internal coherence and the integrity of the festival's
organization, both its inaugural and concluding ceremonies were performed in the same place. This, on the other hand, does not necessarily
mean that the festival was an exclusive prerogative of a single temple. In 2
Kgs 23.9 the refusal of the priests of the high places to come and celebrate
Passover in Jerusalem, staying instead, as the author says, to eat the
unleavened bread among their brethren, could be a simple introductory
cue for the subsequent actions of Josiah, but it can be also argued that the
story has an indirect didactic purpose: to warn all of those who celebrate
Passover outside Jerusalem what destiny eventually awaits them. The
indirect threat could be specifically targeting the Samaritans who indeed
had their own temple which competed with the one in Jerusalem, but it can
be also an indication that there were many other places where people
observed Passover, given that the story refers quite generally to 'high
places' without naming any particular location. Beside Jerusalem and
Gerizim, Passover could have been observed in other places that we do not
know about. They might not have been as renowned as the temples in
Jerusalem and on Gerizim, but the people could have continued to visit
them because they were closer to home and to avoid a prolonged journey
during harvest time. In this respect, as a festival that was observed in more
than one location, Passover was not an exception from the cultic practice
of the ancient Near East. The Sumerian Akitu, for example, was celebrated
in Ur,[35] Nipur, Adab and Uruk.[36]

It should be mentioned here that in addition to the sacrifice during the
first night and the unleavened bread, another ritual was nominally
separated from Passover. The ritual in question is the cutting of the first

34. Pierce 1999: 161–89.
35. The celebration in Ur involved three different locations: at the du-ur sanctuary, in the
Ekinsungal temple of Nanna and at the Ekazida in Gaes, a small town on the outskirts of Ur.
Cohen 1993: 406.
36. Cohen 1993: 401.

sheaves of barley or the feast of Sheaf which is briefly described in Leviticus[37] and only alluded to in Deuteronomy[38] and neither of them strictly connects it with Passover. However, Philo and Josephus[39] provide sufficient details about it to conclude that it was indeed part of Passover. Here is how Philo describes Passover and its three sub-feasts:

> After the New Moon comes the fourth feast, called the Crossing-feast, which the Hebrews in their native tongue call Pascha... With the Crossing-feast he combines one in which the food consumed is of different and unfamiliar kind, namely, the unleavened bread, which also gives its name to the feast... But within the feast there is another feast following directly after the first day. This is called the Sheaf, a name given to it from the ceremony which consists in bringing to the altar a sheaf as a first fruit...[40]

A similar 'splintering' happened to Tabernacles whose original structure in later times was divided on three separate feasts, New Year's feast, the Day of Atonement and Tabernacles.[41] These sub-feasts were a real liturgical 'stretching' that tripled the original duration of the festival. Passover, however, preserved its temporal integrity and the sub-feasts, despite their nominal 'splintering', continued to be celebrated within the seven-day period.

2.2. *Home versus Temple*

The second argument put in support of the dual origin theory is that Passover sacrifice was a family feast, whose original place of observance was the family home and that only after being conjoined with Unleavened Bread did it begin to be performed in a temple. In general, conclusions about the family character of Passover sacrifice are based partly on the legislative text from Exod. 12.1–13[42] and partly on the description of the

---

37. Lev. 23.10–14.
38. Deut. 16.9.
39. Flavius, *Jewish Antiquities* III, 248–51. Philo, *Spec. Leg.* II, 162.
40. Philo, *Spec. Leg.* II, 145–62.
41. Snaith 1947: 150; Segal 1963: 127–28.
42. Exod. 12.1–13. (1) The Lord said to Moses and Aaron in the land of Egypt, (2) This month shall be for you the beginning of months; it shall be the first month of the year for you. (3) Tell all the congregation of Israel that on the tenth day of this month they shall take every man a lamb according to their fathers' houses, a lamb for a household; (4) and if the household is too small for a lamb, then a man and his neighbour next to his house shall take according to the number of persons; according to what each can eat you shall make your count for the lamb. (5) Your lamb shall be without blemish, a male a year old; you shall take it from the sheep or from the goats; (6) and you shall keep it until the fourteenth day of this month, when the whole assembly of the congregation of Israel shall kill their lambs in the evening. (7) Then they shall take some of the blood, and put it on the two doorposts and the lintel of the houses in which they eat them. (8) They shall eat the flesh that night, roasted;

Passover observance on the night before the exodus in Exod. 12.21–23.[43] In both of these texts Passover sacrifice is presented as a home affair with many details regarding the choice of sacrificial animals, the use of the blood, the preparation and consumption of the flesh and finally the 'dress code' required for the occasion. Among them, the most quoted ones as evidence in support for its family character are the expression 'fathers' houses', the place of its performance, and the blood rite.

However, in comparison to other biblical texts referring to Passover, the Exodus passages involving these three details stand out as an exception. In none of the other legislative texts is the family home mentioned as the place to observe the ritual on the first day, nor is the family designated as the supplier of the sacrificial animals, while all of them are completely silent about the blood rite. Leviticus only mentions that on the fourteenth of the first month in the evening is the Lord's Passover, giving no further explanation. In view of Leviticus' sacrificial stipulation for Passover it refers solely to the regular daily fire offering which is to be presented continuously during the whole period of the festival.[44] In a similar way, Numbers also only states that on the fourteenth of the first month is the Lord's passover,[45] but gives more details regarding the burnt offerings offered during the festival. On the first day the offering consists of two young bulls, one ram, seven male one-year-old lambs, and one male goat as a sin offering. The second category of burnt sacrifice which is offered daily for seven days is called 'the food of an offering by fire' and is further described as 'a pleasing odour to the Lord'.[46] In Ezekiel it is stipulated that the prince should be the provider of

---

with unleavened bread and bitter herbs they shall eat it. (9) Do not eat it raw or boiled with water, but roasted, its head with its legs and its inner parts. (10) And you shall let none of it remain until the morning, anything that remains until the morning you shall burn. (11) In this manner you shall eat it: your loins girded, your sandals on your feet and your staff in your hand; and you shall eat it in haste. It is the Lord's passover. (12) For I will pass through the land of Egypt that night, and I will smite all the first-born in the land of Egypt, both man and beast; and on all the gods of Egypt I will execute a judgement: I am the Lord. (13) The blood shall be the sign for you, upon the houses where you are; and when I see the blood, I will pass over you, and no plague shall fall upon you to destroy you, when I smite the land of Egypt.

43. Exod. 12.21–23: (21) Then Moses called all the elders of Israel, and said to them, 'Select lambs for yourselves according to your families, and kill the passover lamb. (22) Take a bunch of hyssop and dip it in the blood which is in the basin, and touch the lintel and the two doorposts with the blood which is in the basin; and none of you shall go out of the door of his house until morning. (23) For the Lord will pass through to sally the Egyptians; and when he sees the blood on the lintel and on the two doorposts, the Lord will pass over the door, and will not allow the destroyer to enter your houses to slay you.

44. Lev. 23.5, 8.

45. Num. 28.16.

46. Num. 28.16–25.

all sacrificial animals. On the first day a young bull should be offered as a sin offering, while on other days of the festival the prince should provide seven young bulls and seven rams daily and a male goat as a sin offering.[47]

In none of these texts is it mentioned that the flesh of the ritual animals should be consumed within the houses; neither could any of the accounted sacrifices be interpreted as being offered by every family for it is quite clear that apart from the royal family very few families would be able to fulfil, for example, the sacrificial obligation from Numbers. It is quite obvious that all of them refer to a temple practice. Furthermore, there is no mention of any particular sacrificial ritual on the first day of the festival. In the texts we find the terms Lord's Passover[48] or feast of the passover,[49] the meaning of which in the context is obscure. They could denote the whole festival, but also the particular rite on its first day. The only exception from this string of legislative texts, which show complete indifference to any peculiar ritual as part of Passover, are the ordinances in Deuteronomy. Deuteronomy explicitly mentions 'passover sacrifice' as the unique feature of the festival. However, its observance is strictly connected with the temple where the animal is killed, prepared and consumed.[50] Underlining the importance of the temple as the site where the rite on the first day of the festival takes place is also the prohibition to leave its precincts until the next morning.[51]

The same ignorance regarding Passover sacrifice as a ritual with family character appears in narratives about individual celebrations. Apart from the ritual before exodus when the members of the families were both the providers of the ritual animals and their sacrificers, in other descriptions of actual observances the Passover animals are usually mentioned as being offered on behalf of the present people[52] or as being distributed according to the groupings of fathers' houses.[53] Most commonly the sacrifices are provided by the royal family, high officials of the temple and the Levites.[54] They are never killed by laymen; animals killed and offered as Passover sacrifices include lambs, kids and bulls.[55] And the celebration, including its first day, is always held on a sacred ground[56] or in the temple.[57]

47. Ezek. 45.21–23.
48. Lev. 23.5; Num. 28.16.
49. Ezek. 45.21.
50. Deut. 16.7.
51. Deut. 16.8; Haran 1985: 343.
52. Ezra 6.20b.
53. 2 Chron. 35.12.
54. 2 Chron. 30.24; 35.7.
55. 2 Chron. 30.24; 35.7–9.
56. Moses' Passover on Sinai, Num. 9.1–5; Joshua's in Gilgal, Josh. 5.10.
57. In 2 Chron. 8.12–13 Solomon keeps the appointed feasts in the temple. Hezekiah's and Josiah's Passovers are also kept in the temple. 2 Chron. 30.15–16; 35.1–2. Ezra's Passover happens only after the dedication of the temple which points to a close link between the two. Ezra 6.16–21.

From the picture painted by non-Exodus texts one might rightfully ask about the reasons of scholars to postulate that exactly those features of Exodus Passover which cannot be found in any other biblical Passover text are an illustration of the true character of the ritual on the first day of the festival. The answer to this question is that they were interpreted without taking into account that the primary function of the story of the Exodus Passover is to be an aetiology. It was assumed that the ritual was simply given a historical explanation without actually considering how much the aetiological function and consequently the setting and the circumstances of the story rule the imagery of its features. As we shall see, when the three distinguishing elements of Exodus Passover – the expression 'father's houses', the home as the place where the ritual is performed and finally the application of the blood – are analysed bearing in mind the aetiological function of the story, it becomes clear that they are just the author's interpretation of how the Passover must have been observed in the absence of a temple. In other words, their nature is functional rather than structural.

In order to have a proper understanding of the meaning which the idiom 'fathers' houses' has in the context of Exodus Passover we have to turn to anthropology and its explanation of kinship units. According to Keesing,[58] when dealing with kinship units one should have a clear understanding that the same unit can refer actually to two quite different kinds of membership. Being a member of a unit that has the character of a social category means to belong to an essentially abstract grouping based on a certain socially relevant feature that is shared by all the members. In this sense, every kinship unit is a social category. However, kinship units can also operate as a social group, which means that its members are part of an active, everyday functioning unit consisting of real people who interact among themselves, whose position in the group is defined by their gender, age, and so on. A kinship unit that has the characteristic of a social group operates as a kind of 'action' or 'task' group and belonging to such units means real and active membership. In contrast, belonging to a social category mostly means a passive and abstract membership. As social categories, kinship units mostly provide the parameters for belonging to a certain group, but it is the social group that is the real, everyday, effective unit. Depending on the circumstances, units that predominantly function as social categories might, for a limited time, take upon the role of being an 'action group'. Most often, however, their only way of involvement with the lives of their members is entitlement to a certain claim, such as a common ancestor.

In the biblical texts that in some way refer to or involve kinship units, these two distinct modalities of membership are easily recognized. With respect to the different way in which the membership manifests in everyday life, clans and tribes belong almost without exception to social categories,

---

58. Keesing 1975: 213–15.

while fathers' houses most commonly have the character of a group. They are not just the smallest units in the hierarchy of biblical kinship organization, but also the ones that are effective. In the Old Testament, affairs that require a certain measure of practical organization are almost never done at the level of tribes or clans. For example, real numbers of male heads for the census in Numbers 1 are not provided by clans or tribes, but by fathers' houses. Referring to the inheritance of Reuben's and Gad's tribes, Moses says that it was received by their fathers' houses.[59]

In Exod. 12.3 the expression 'fathers' houses' stands for efficacious rather than kinship associations. That the accent is on the effectiveness of the group performing the ritual is clear from the biblical text itself because straight after referring to fathers' houses, it also designates households as the would-be participating groups. In contrast to fathers' houses which include only members that are by blood or marriage related to the patriarch who is the kinship link among them, households might include persons that are in no kinship relationship to the head of the family. But they are indeed a very effective social group. The text additionally strengthens this aspect of the association performing the ritual by requiring neighbouring households to join up if the number of persons is too small for the whole lamb to be consumed during a single night.[60] The focus of the author is obviously not on granting the family members the exclusive privilege to perform the ritual, but rather on the adequate number of persons that can effectively eat a whole lamb in a very short time. His primary concern is to have a proper performance of the ritual and the 'father's house' is just one among the groups that can effectively complete the task.[61] From this perspective it is clear why he begins the call with 'all the congregation of Israel',[62] but ends it with requiring joint households. Israel as such, as one large, all-embracing kinship unit, is an abstract entity and the performance of the ritual has to occur through social groups such as fathers' houses or households. In the Exodus text, observance of Passover is a group and not a family affair. And in this respect it still pertains to the idea of a gathering, a holy convocation or holy assembly, as is described in other biblical texts.[63]

---

59. Num. 34.14: for the tribe of the sons of Reuben by fathers' houses and the tribe of the sons of Gad by their fathers' houses have received their inheritance and also the half-tribe of Manasseh.

60. Exod. 12.4.

61. D. Bergant, for example, who discusses only the kinship aspect of the expressions 'father's house' and 'household' completely misses this point and concludes that the reference to the neighbouring household is perplexing since it refers to people with no blood ties and even more so because the most likely neighbours in the particular setting of Exodus legislation would be the Egyptians. Bergant 1995: 51.

62. Exod. 12.3.

63. Lev. 23.7; Num. 28.18.

The other two elements of the Exodus Passover that are not found in any other biblical text referring to the festival, but are nevertheless used as evidence in support of its dual origin, are the blood rite and the house as the site where the flesh of the animal is consumed.[64] The basic assumption is that the rite had apotropaic qualities and that the blood was applied to the family residence in order to protect the family from evil, demonic or suchlike powers and influences.[65] However, when we take into consideration the specific setting in which this Passover sacrifice takes place the assumption about the protective powers of the rite is untenable.

As we have seen earlier, the members of the group performing the ritual do not have to belong to a single family. Consequently, neither is the house in which the flesh of the sacrificial animal is to be consumed necessarily a family home for each member of the group. The blood, however, is not applied on the doorposts and the lintel of every Israelite home, but only on those that are part of the house where the group performs the ritual eating. 'Then they shall take some of the blood, and put it on the two doorposts and the lintel of the houses in which they eat them.'[66]

The house on which the blood is smeared in the Exodus texts does not represent a family residence. Neither is the application of blood an apotropaic rite intended to protect the family members. The house represents an enclosed space, while, in this case, the blood is a cleansing, purifying agent, whose application on the entrance temporarily transforms the inside of the house into a hallowed ground, a temple. Philo's remark that during Passover every dwelling is 'invested like the outward semblance and dignity of a temple'[67] only confirms that the homes in which the Exodus Passover is performed play the role of surrogate temples. The application of blood by smearing and sprinkling, particularly in combination with hyssop, has the power to purge impurities,[68] and Leviticus abounds in similar examples.[69] In order to cleanse the temple at the beginning of the year Ezekiel requires a very similar rite to that in

64. Exod. 12.7, 22–23.

65. Gray 1925: 337–82; De Vaux 1965: II, 492; Ringgren 1966: 186–87; Zeitlin 1984: 86; Levinson 1997: 58.

66. Exod. 12.7.

67. Philo, *Spec. Leg.* II, 148.

68. Ps. 51.7: Purge me with hyssop, and I shall be clean; wash me, and I shall be whiter than snow.

69. Lev. 14.6–7: (6) He shall take the living bird with the cedarwood and the scarlet stuff and the hyssop, and dip them and the living bird in the blood of the bird that was killed over the running water; (7) and he shall sprinkle it seven times upon him who is to be cleansed of leprosy; then he shall pronounce him clean, and shall let the living bird go into the open field. Lev. 14.52: Thus he shall cleanse the house with the blood of the bird, and with the running water, and with the living bird, and with the cedarwood and hyssop and scarlet stuff. According to Gorman, this holds true both for rituals of atonement and rituals of cleansing. Gorman 1990: 76–77, 131–35.

Exodus Passover.[70] Josephus also interprets the blood rite in Egypt as a purifying act.[71]

There is yet another reason why the blood rite does not have anything to do with protection. Yahweh does not need any signs to exclude the Israelites from the plague he brings upon the Egyptians. In previous plagues, he excludes them from being swarmed by flies,[72] spares their cattle[73] and them from boils,[74] hail[75] and even from darkness[76] and for none of these miracles does he need a visible sign to be able to make the distinction. Why would he need such a sign in the case of killing the first-born? The purpose of the blood on the houses is not to exclude the Israelites, but to make a boundary dividing the stage of the tenth plague drama and Passover ritual into a sacred and profane space.

The peculiar features of Passover sacrifice in Exodus are ruled by the circumstances of the situation in which the author places the Israelites. They are the result of the author's envisioning of how the ritual on the first day of the festival should be performed without a temple while still pertaining to the requirements of its performance in reality. Their meaning in the context of exodus does not contradict the description of the ritual in other biblical texts. It is only the best translation within the particular context of the narrative of the ritual's collective character and the necessity to be performed in a sanctified space.

It is important to point out that in the times immediately before the destruction of the Jerusalem temple in 70 CE most of the particular rituals of Exodus Passover, the selection of lamb on the tenth day, smearing of the blood on the entrance to the house and eating in haste,[77] were not performed. The rabbis of the Mishnah believed they were abandoned because they were part of the specific 'Passover of Egypt'.[78] And they were certainly right in the sense that when there was a proper temple there was no need for this kind of Passover. The only part of the Exodus Passover that was presumably preserved was the eating of the flesh within the

---

70. Ezek. 45.18–19. (18) Thus says the Lord GOD: In the first month, on the first day of the month, you shall take a young bull without blemish, and cleanse the sanctuary. (19) The priest shall take some of the blood of the sin offering and put it on the doorposts of the temple, the four corners of the ledge of the altar and the posts of the gate of the inner court.

71. Josephus, *Antiquities* II, 312.

72. Exod. 8.22–23.

73. Exod. 8.4.

74. Exod. 9.11.

75. Exod. 9.26.

76. Exod. 10.22–23.

77. Exod. 12.3, 7.

78. The Mishnah, *Pesaḥim* 9.5. Neusner 1988: 247. Although it is not clear why because Yahweh ordains it for eternity. Exod. 12.14: This day shall be for you a memorial day, and you shall keep it as a feast to the Lord; throughout your generations you shall observe it as an ordinance for ever.

houses. However, in the years preceding 70 CE the Jerusalem temple was already a very strong religious centre and the transfer of the ritualized eating of the flesh of the sacrificial animal from the temple to houses was due to the large crowds that could not be accommodated within the temple precinct.[79] For many of the pilgrims those houses certainly were not family dwellings. And, as Josephus testifies, the groups performing the eating were not families either, but associations[80] of no less than ten people.[81] The inherent sanctity of the space where the ritual eating was to take place was, nevertheless, preserved. The whole area within the walls of Jerusalem was regarded as a sacred place. Limbs of Passover sacrifice that protruded outside the walls of the city had to be cut off.[82]

If the Passover sacrifice as a clearly family affair cannot be found in Palestine, can we perhaps assume that the people in exile or in diaspora performed it in the manner described in the Exodus legislation? In the Bible, there are two major events in Israelite history that serve as powerful metaphors or, as Carroll says, are 'the two sides or faces of the myth that shapes the subtext of the narratives and rhetoric of the Hebrew Bible'.[83] One of them is the exodus, the other one the exile. However, between these two metaphors there is a difference with respect to the historical experience from which they could have sprung. Exodus seems to have derived from nowhere since it seems that no event like the sojourn in Egypt and the subsequent departure from it ever took place. It is a kind of floating metaphor without anchorage in reality. P. Davies cautiously suggests that the exodus story perhaps echoes the experience of the Israelite soldiers who were planted in Egypt by the Assyrians and were later harassed by the locals, as the Elephantine letters demonstrate, and who might have returned to Palestine during Persian rule.[84] However, unless it exemplified an experience that was more commonly shared, it seems quite unlikely that an episodic affair affecting a handful of people would be elevated to the status of a national myth. The soldiers' misfortunes or any similar event might have given outward shape to that experience, but it is the commonality of it that gave it the skeleton on which the episode could grow into a myth.

In contrast to the exodus, the exile was anchored in reality. However, while the exodus metaphor is couched in an elaborate pseudo-historical narrative, the exile is shrouded in complete silence. No narrative deals with this period and, as Thompson remarks, one cannot escape wondering

---

79. The late apocryphal work *The Book of Jubilees* demands the flesh of the Passover sacrifice to be consumed in the temple court. Jub. 45.15.
80. Josephus, *Antiquities* III, 248.
81. Josephus, *The Jewish War* VI, 423.
82. The Mishnah, *Pesaḥim* 7.12. Neusner 1988: 244.
83. Carroll 1998: 63.
84. Davies 1992: 119.

why the Bible is so uninterested in the life of the exiled people after the fall of Jerusalem.[85] We will not attempt here to clarify the details of the historical 'exile' of the Israelites and give answers to questions such as how it happened or how many times it happened, what was the number of deported people and who were the people that 'returned from exile'. It suffices to quote Thompson's statement that the exile tradition reflects the 'imperial policies from the Assyrian through to the Roman period'[86] and his epigrammatical conclusion 'No, the problem is not whether there was ever a historical exile; nor has it ever been that the Bible's stories are not believable. There was exile ... often.'[87] Exiles indeed happened and not all of them were forceful. However, both the people that were forcefully moved and those who moved of their own volition knew what it meant to be resettled, to 'be exiled', to be planted into an alien and most probably hostile environment. Exile as such did not represent a unique historical event, but rather a specific social condition, an experience that was known not just in Palestine proper but throughout the Mediterranean region.

The biblical sojourn in Egypt and what we can reasonably assume was the reality of the widely shared exilic experience have many details in common. We shall mention just the most conspicuous ones: both situations involve two different ethnic groups or rather the indigenous people who are in the majority and migrants who are in the minority. In both cases, the minority group, the Israelites in the story, and the newly arrived people of the real exile, is in an adverse position and is the threatened group. The threat comes from a central authority. In the exodus that authority is embodied in the character of the Pharaoh; in the case of the real exile that authority is represented by the imperial policies of deportation and resettlement.

These coincidences are perhaps an indication that it was this 'exilic experience' and its commonality that were the fertile ground for the rise of a powerful national myth that begins with sojourn in an alien country. However, with respect to Passover sacrifice and its Exodus legislation it is obvious that it is this notion of being in an alien country that controls its performance. The place of its observance, the house, reflects the idea that the festival is performed in a foreign country, in 'exilic conditions' and, therefore, also outside of its legitimate place, the sacred ground of the patron god of Israel. In such circumstances, as an enclosed space, 'house' is the closest substitute for the god's house, the temple.

The only place outside of Palestine about which we have some information regarding Passover is Elephantine in Egypt where the Jewish military colony apparently observed it during the fifth century BCE since it

---

85. Thompson 1999: 219.
86. Thompson 1999: 214.
87. Thompson 1999: 217.

is mentioned in two ostraca and a papyrus.[88] However, the colony also had a temple dedicated to Yaho, a fact which makes it possible that the festival had the same form as in Palestine. As to the manner in which it was performed when there was no temple, and furthermore whether it was celebrated at all, we are actually in complete darkness. The book of Tobit, which recounts the adventures of the descendent of an Israelite taken captive by the Assyrians and transported to Nineveh, perhaps offers some clues as to the form important temple observances took in the absence of a Jewish shrine. It mentions that the Feast of Pentecost (Weeks), another prominently temple festival, was celebrated at home.[89] If it was ever observed in the diaspora, Passover could have suffered a similar change. The lack of a typically Jewish cult place or perhaps the recognition of the authority of the Palestinian temples could have been good reasons to transfer the Passover observance to family houses, while the role of the priests in sacrificing the animal and in the handling of its blood could have been taken over by the family members. The changes may have been mere adaptations of the ritual to new conditions but also preventative measures against amalgamation with the local population. Being without their own temples[90] meant that the Jews were supposed to worship in alien temples which would have, on the other hand, most certainly contributed to the process of their cultural assimilation.[91] Given the fact that, in the places where they dwelt either as exiles or as diaspora, local festivals were celebrated at the time of the spring equinox when Passover was also observed, the restriction of the Passover sacrifice to family houses could have developed as a particular kind of 'ritual of resistance', as D.L. Smith calls cultic practices idiosyncratic to the Israelites in exile;[92] a ritual which would give the Jews a feeling of being different from the host nation and its religious practices. However, as Bokser's discussion on the origins of seder demonstrates, as a festival with an entirely family character and very much as a 'ritual of resistance' Passover developed only after the destruction of the Jerusalem temple.[93]

88. The two ostraca mention 'passover', while the papyrus, although very damaged, mentions leaven in connection with the month of Nisan and dates such as fourteenth, fifteenth and twenty-first, all of which are indicative of Passover.

89. Tob. 2.1: When I arrived home and my wife Anna and my son Tobias were restored to me, at the feast of Pentecost, which is the sacred festival of the seven weeks, a good dinner was prepared for me and I sat down to eat.

90. The question of whether the Israelites had their own temples in diaspora is an issue whose complexity surpasses the scope of this work. Apart from the temples in Elephantine and Leontopolis no other temples outside Palestine are known to have existed.

91. The Letter of Jeremiah allegedly sent to the exiles in Babylon most vividly expresses this fear of amalgamation.

92. Smith 1989: 139–49.

93. Bokser 1974: 90.

2.3. *Pastoral versus Agricultural*

Up to this point we have managed to challenge two major arguments on which some theories of Passover as a combination of two independent feasts are based. However, there is still the argument that the Passover sacrifice and the Feast of the Unleavened Bread stemmed from different segments of Israelite society, namely, from the pastoral and the agricultural, which is an idea that still may raise doubts regarding the coherence between the ritual on the first day and the rest of the festival.

In the majority of scholarly discussions on Passover that elaborate on its alleged dual origins, the essential notion is that the features of Passover sacrifice reflect the non-sedentary way of life, while the Feast of the Unleavened Bread allegedly deals with the concerns of sedentary people. Most often this notion is the result of the now-antiquated theory about the nomadic past of the Israelites. However, there are still scholars who believe that Passover sacrifice reflects, if not exactly the nomadic, then the pastoral rhythm of life in transhumance conditions.[94] There is no doubt that such an explanation would carry some weight if the ancient Near Eastern cultures, including the Israelite culture, made a clear distinction between the two segments of their societies, namely, the pastoral and the agricultural, or if they had a strict social stratification along occupational lines similar to the Indian caste system. That, however, was not the case. Farmers and shepherds were mutually dependant and lived in a symbiosis.[95] The reflection of that symbiotic life can be found in the myths and rituals of the ancient Near East in which it is actually impossible to distinguish between the originally pastoral and the originally agricultural elements. Their gods and rites were quite ambivalent in this respect. For example, Tammuz, the Babylonian vegetation god, was often addressed as 'shepherd'. The same term was used to denote the rulers of the predominantly agricultural population of the region. In Egypt, the white bull was the sacred animal of Min, the Egyptian god of fertility, whose main festival opened the agrarian season of harvesting. Daily sacrifices to the gods of the Babylonian Uruk included beer, loaves of barley and emmer flour, dates, figs, bulls, rams and birds.[96] The same was true for Ugarit. Sacrificial lists include wine, different animals, loaves, flour, and so on.[97]

In Passover we find the same kind of ambiguity regarding pastoral and agricultural elements. In Exod. 34.25–26 we find the regulation on Passover sacrifice, which is presumed to represent a pastoral ritual and

94.   Albertz 1994: 35.
95.   Thompson 1994: 67.
96.   Pritchard 1969: 343–44.
97.   Del Olmo Lete 1999: 87–166.

as such to be essentially indifferent to the concerns of the farmers, to be alternating in the text with that of the first fruits and without a clear distinction between the two.[98] The same alternating structure between animal and first fruit offerings appears in Exod. 23.18–19. If these verses reflect any other concern apart from ensuring a proper performance of the two rituals it is then the concern of the community in general.

It is sometimes regarded that the choice of an animal for the sacrifice on the first day of Passover is evidence that the rite was of pastoral origin because shepherds in line with their occupation prefer animals as offerings, while farmers favour sacrifices of vegetable origin.[99] With respect to the type, all the civilizations of the ancient Near East had considerable animal sacrifices and the preference for an animal as a ritual offering did not have anything to do with whether the community was mainly engaged in farming or animal husbandry. In the story of Cain and Abel,[100] when Yahweh accepts Abel's firstling but is indifferent to Cain's fruits of the ground, the animal sacrifice is represented as the divine choice. Yahweh's preference, however, is not based on the fact that Abel is a shepherd. It is rather the blood, the carrier of life, for which it is very hard to find an equivalent in the world of plants, that is the reason behind his selection. Wine that was sometimes regarded as a substitution for blood and a symbol of life,[101] yet a product of vegetable origin, was never in that capacity used in sacrifices.

In the Leviticus it is said 'For the life of every creature is the blood of it'.[102] In the Bible, blood is synonymous with life,[103] which is on the other hand Yahweh's exclusive prerogative. Therefore the Israelites are forbidden to eat blood.[104] People who dare to drink of this nectar of life,

---

98.   Exod. 34.25–26. (25) You shall not offer the blood of my sacrifice with leaven; neither shall the sacrifice of the feast of passover be left until the morning. (26) The first of the first fruits of your ground you shall bring to the house of the Lord your God. You shall not boil a kid in its mother's milk.

99.   'The Sheaf is the offering of an *agricultural* community and not of a nomadic community; the Paschal victim, a slain animal, though it could be, and was, offered after the Hebrews became agriculturalists, is an equally natural offering for a nomadic community' (Gray 1925: 343). 'According to ancient nomadic custom the Israelites ... would offer chiefly animal sacrifice and specially that of beasts from their flocks. In Egypt the sacrifice of whole animals including sheep and goats was not completely unknown, although it was not very usual; by preference a vegetable offering was made along with poultry and pieces of meat' (Noth 1962: 78).

100.   Gen. 4.3–5.

101.   Deut. 32.14.

102.   Lev. 17.14; Deut. 12.23.

103.   Gen. 9.4: Only you shall not eat flesh with its life, that is, its blood. Ps. 72.14: From oppression and violence he redeems their life; and precious is their blood in his sight.

104.   Gen. 9.4; Lev. 3.17; 7.26; 17.12, 14; 19.26; Deut. 12.16, 23.

befitting only gods, are to be cut off from the community.[105] The blood of animals which are killed for food has to be poured on the ground[106] while the blood of sacrificial animals has to be thrown against[107] or poured out at the base of the altar,[108] the symbol of Yahweh's divinely abode. Blood as an essence of life is Yahweh's divine right.

Yahweh's exclusive right to physical manifestations of life also play an important role in understanding Yahweh's demand for consecration of firstlings and firstborn, an ordinance which appears in connection with Passover and on which many discussions of the alleged pastoral origin of Passover sacrifice rely for support. The basic assumption is that Exod. 13.11–15[109] and 34.18–20[110] reflect the original purpose of Passover sacrifice as a consecration of firstlings.[111] Whether the animal sacrificed on the first night of Passover was ever a firstling or not is impossible to glean from the texts. Perhaps the singular form, 'the Passover lamb',[112] constantly used in the Bible to actually denote numerous and heterogeneous animals hints that they were all marked by some fundamental characteristic common to all of them. It could be argued that they were all real firstlings, but it is equally possible that they were all just male animals, no older than one year, as the regulation in Exod. 12.5 stipulates, or that they were in some other way comprehended as a single sacrifice. However, it should be noted that not all Passover regulations are limited to firstlings. Some embrace all categories of first issues, irrespective of

105.   Lev. 7.27; 17.10, 14.

106.   Lev. 17.13; Deut. 12.16; 15.23.

107.   Exod. 24.6; 29.15–16, 19; Lev. 1.5, 10–11; 3.2, 6, 13.

108.   Exod. 29.12; Lev. 4.7, 18, 25, 30, 34; 8.15; 9.9; Deut. 12.27.

109.   Exod. 13.11–15. (11) And when the Lord brings you into the land of Canaanites, as he swore to you and your fathers, and shall give it to you, (12) you shall set apart to the Lord all that first opens the womb. All the firstlings of your cattle that are males shall be the Lord's. (13) Every firstling of an ass you shall redeem with a lamb, or if you will not redeem it you shall break its neck. Every first-born of man among your sons you shall redeem. (14) And when in time to come your son asks you 'What does this mean?' you shall say to him, 'By strength of hand the Lord brought us out of Egypt, from the house of bondage. (15) For when Pharaoh stubbornly refused to let us go, the Lord slew all the first-born of man and the first-born of cattle. Therefore I sacrifice to the Lord all the males that first open the womb; but all the first-born of my sons I redeem.'

110.   Exod. 34.18–20. (18) The feast of unleavened bread you shall keep. Seven days you shall eat unleavened bread, as I commanded you, at the time appointed in the month Abib; for in the month of Abib you came out of Egypt. (19) All that opens the womb is mine, all your male cattle, the firstlings of cow and sheep. (20) The firstling of an ass you shall redeem with a lamb, or if you will not redeem it you shall break its neck. All the first-born of your sons you shall redeem. And none shall appear before me empty.

111.   Wellhausen 1885: 83–94; Pedersen 1959: 398; Beer 1912: 23.

112.   Exod. 12.21; 2 Chron. 30.15, 17; 35.1, 6, 11, 13; Ezra 6.20.

whether they come from animals, humans or plants,[113] which is certainly an indication that the Passover sacrifice did not arise just from the pastoral segment. The verses in Exod. 13.11–13 which mention only the consecration of firstlings and firstborn are part of the exodus narrative, and by emphasizing solely those two categories the author merely parallels Yahweh's own words regarding the final plague that killed Egyptian firstborn of men and animal.[114] In Exod. 34.25–26,[115] for example, the Passover sacrifice appears in close relation to the first fruits. And this relation does not seem to be accidental since the first fruits mentioned in the text are none other than the first sheaves of barley that were ceremonially cut during the second night of Passover[116] and consequently presented in the temple.

What scholars usually miss in their attempts to understand the nature of the connection between the Passover sacrifice and firstlings and firstborn is that the Bible connects Passover with all categories of first issues, those of humans, those of animals and those of plants. This connection with first issues in general, however, undermines the claim that the original purpose of the Passover sacrifice was the consecration of animal and human firstborn. Exod. 13.1–2, 12–13, where firstlings and firstborn are stipulated to belong to Yahweh, cannot be taken to represent legislation strictly for Passover because, as mentioned earlier, the connection between their consecration and Passover is secondary, through the story of the tenth plague. The main focus of the legislation is actually on the reasons for consecrating the firstlings and firstborn to Yahweh.[117] Apart from this, there is the requirement in Exod. 22.30 which overrides the eventual consecration of firstlings on Passover since it stipulates that they are to be offered on the eighth day after their birth. The only consecration to have most likely taken place during Passover, but only after the Passover sacrifice ritual was over, was that of the 'first of the first fruits of the ground' mentioned in Exod. 34.26.

However, although the purpose of the Passover sacrifice ritual does not seem to be consecration, it cannot be denied that first issues were in some way associated with the festival itself. To discover the nature of that association and the light it can shed on Passover and its purpose before its transformation into a commemorative festival, it is necessary to examine the meaning of firstlings, firstborn and first fruits in the Bible.

---

113. Exod. 34.18–26.
114. Exod. 13.15.
115. Exod. 34.25–26. (25) You shall not offer the blood of my sacrifice with leaven; neither shall the sacrifice of the feast of passover be left until the morning. (26) The first of the first fruits of your ground you shall bring to the house of the Lord your God. You shall not boil a kid in its mother's milk.
116. The Mishnah, *Menaḥot* 10.3. Neusner 1988: 753–54.
117. De Vaux 1965: II, 489; Childs 1974: 195.

Most often the meaning of firstlings and firstborn is discussed separately from that of first fruits. R.J. Smith, for example, connected the special interest that Yahweh shows for human and animal firstborn with the intrinsic holiness of the kin's blood that, as he believed, was comprehended to flow in its purest and strongest form in firstborn for which firstlings were consequently the most appropriate sacrificial substitute.[118] First fruits, according to him, never had any holiness about them because only a small portion of them were consecrated by being placed on the altar. And the purpose of that ritual was to make the whole crop lawful for human consumption.[119] It is true that the purpose of Sheaf, 'the first of the first fruit of the ground', was primarily to release the new crop for human consumption.[120] The Mishnah describes how the markets were full of parched grain after the waving of the first sheaf.[121] What Smith fails to heed, though, is that all three kinds of first issues had to be offered to Yahweh. Human firstborn were redeemed, firstlings were sacrificed and first fruits were placed on the altar. In that respect they were all holy. The insignificance of the quantity of the grain offering did not make it less holy compared to the firstlings. How can one otherwise offer the crop unless through a symbolic portion? The point is that all three categories of first issues were marked by an intrinsic holiness by the mere fact of being the very first. They were 'the first to open the womb', to use Yahweh's dramatic expression, and that vital first opening was a manifest confirmation of fertility, of giving life. The first opening of the womb was obvious evidence of future procreation and new offspring that would ensure the survival of the community.[122] In this sense there was no difference between the opening of the womb of the earth and the opening of the womb of animals and humans and their respective first fruits. They were all equally important and the legislation regarding their consecration reflects the main preoccupation of all ancient cultures, namely, fertility in general.

In the Bible, fertility is, like in the case of life, Yahweh's prerogative. He is the one who decides which womb will be opened and which one will remain closed. Sarah, Rebekah, Rachel and many other biblical female characters remain barren until Yahweh decides to make them fertile.[123] By demanding that all firstborn of any category, animal, human or plant be consecrated to him, Yahweh only re-affirms his authority over the domain

118.   Smith 1907: 465.
119.   Smith 1907: 241.
120.   Lev. 23.14.
121.   The Mishnah, *Menahot* 10.5, A, D. Neusner 1988: 755.
122.   In Philo's words: 'Yet even parents have their first-born male children consecrated as a first-fruit, a thank offering for the blessing of parenthood realized in the present and the hopes of fruitful increase in future.' *Spec. Leg.* I, 138.
123.   Gen. 18.13–14; 25.21; 30.22.

of fertility.[124] From this perspective, it is clear that the governing idea behind the connection between Passover sacrifice and firstlings and firstborn in Exodus legislation, regardless of how indirect and secondary that connection might be, is fertility. On the night of Passover in Egypt Yahweh implicitly appears in the aspect of a fertility god. That hidden meaning of Yahweh in the story of the tenth plague, on the other hand, suggests that before it was transformed into a commemoration Passover belonged to the category of festivals dedicated to the fertility cult and the gods and myths of that particular cult.

The world of the ancient Near East had numerous cults. Among them, one of the most important and certainly the oldest was the one dedicated to fertility. Its antiquity is attested by numerous Palaeolithic female statues, very often without any face, but with prominent breasts and genitals which undoubtedly display the early human fascination with the miracle of birth and woman as a giver of life.[125] Inscriptions and texts, in which fertility is presented as the greatest blessing and sterility as the greatest affliction, demonstrate its enormous importance. The treaty stelae invoke the gods to strike the violator with destruction of his seed, with drought, infertility of the livestock and similar calamities, while to the one who respects it numerous sons and the like are promised.[126] In this regard Palestine was no exception. Small nude female figurines were among the most frequent archaeological finds in the region. A variety of explanations are offered as to their purpose,[127] but their nudity and protruding breasts in combination at times with an infant almost speak for themselves. In the biblical texts, fertility is the ultimate way in which the blessing of Yahweh is manifested.[128] In return for obeying the Lord's commandment, Deuteronomy 28 promises to the Israelites that the Lord will love them, bless them and multiply them; he will also bless the fruit of their body and the fruit of their ground, grain, wine and oil; he will increase the cattle and the young of the flock. The punishment for disobeying has a reverse direction.

Very often the cult of fertility has been connected solely with the idea of procreation. However, its conceptual base is actually much broader and includes everything that brings, maintains and promises life. Its central notion is life and its sustenance. The interest in fertility is immanent to man as a natural being, as a being of instincts. In defining the interrelation

---

124. According to J. Levenson who maintains that sacrifice of firstborn was a norm in ancient Israel rather than a deviation, Yahweh's exclusive right to firstborn is also manifest in biblical stories about Ishamel and Isaac, Joseph and his ten older brothers, Esau and Jacob, in which the younger son gains the birthright of the older. Levenson 1993: 55–61.

125. Bonanno 1985.

126. Van Rooy 1985.

127. Van der Toorn 2002: 56–57.

128. Gen. 1.22, 28; 9.1; 17.20; 22.17.

between man, his impulses and his actions, A. Gehlen says that, in view of human deficiencies, it is clear that man must perceive in order to act and must act in order to survive.[129] The fertility cult and everything that it included, rituals, myths and festivals, covered this sphere of perception and the sphere of directed action. It represented the perceived and conscious projection of the instinct to survive.

Throughout millennia, from Ur to Egypt, various fertility deities, both male and female, were honoured and their festivals celebrated with special attention. At the level of phenomenal appearances, the heterogeneous multitude of gods and goddesses and their festivals seem to elude every schematization since each of them had some particular trait which distinguished it from the rest. Essentially, however, they were not much different from each other since they were all expressing the same, and at the same time the most important, concern of the ancient world: how to survive.

If we consider the importance Passover had for the shaping of the Israelite Yahwistic cultural and religious tradition, we shall find that the same kind of extremely high degree of significance was assigned to it as was in polytheistic religions to fertility. The first Passover in Egypt is represented as the key moment and the turning point in the history of the Israelites, when they collectively, by divine choice and divine action, as a people, became the chosen people and the delivered people. Passover on the night of the exodus is a culminating point towards which the whole previous history of the patriarchs is directed. Until that crucial night, Yahweh interacts only with individuals, Abraham, Isaac, Joseph and their individual destinies. The Passover night in Egypt subsumes that history of individuals and represents its climax. The role of Yahweh's chosen person, the executor of his will and the occupant of history is from that night transferred from individuals to the people of Israel. The Passover night and the killing of the Egyptian firstborn are a particular theophany of Yahweh before every Israelite. Passover laws in the context of the exodus are, in fact, the first laws that Yahweh gives to Israel as a collective being. On the other hand, such crucial, life-giving importance that the Passover story has continually had for the shaping and maintaining of the Jewish national consciousness could have been possible only if its predecessor had belonged to the same life-giving category of pagan ideas, namely, if it had been related to the fertility cult.

2.4. *Calendric versus Seasonal*

In contrast to the majority of scholars, both Segal and Engnell maintained that Passover was never an amalgam of two separate feasts, but rather an

---

129.   Gehlen 1988: 43.

Israelite version of a New Year festival. However, their views widely differ with respect to the character of Passover as a New Year feast. Engnell regards it as a seasonal festival whose main purpose was maintaining fertility and establishment of cosmos, believing that the reciting of the prayer for dew and the Song of Songs which are still part of the Passover liturgy reflect the theme of the dying and resurrecting god.[130] Segal, however, argues that Passover was a calendar New Year festival primarily associated with the date of the spring equinox and that as such did not have any correlation with the vegetation processes or the season in which it took place.[131] According to Segal, the god to whom Passover was dedicated was not a fertility god in any form, but an exclusive national deity of Israel.[132] In order to see how valid are Segal's claims about Passover's pre-eminently calendric character, given that he, like Engnell, views Passover as a whole, but in contrast both to Engnell's claim and our findings from the previous chapter denies its connection with the fertility cult, it is necessary to investigate that claim against the background of ancient Near Eastern cultures' methods for reckoning the passage of time and the character of their calendars.

In the modern calendar, the motions of the Earth and its correlation with the sun provide the fundamental principle for dividing time into units of years and days. However, for the ancient astronomers of the Near East who were familiar only with the geocentric theory and who observed the sky with the naked eye, how to calculate, divide and record the passage of time were complex problems. Since the motions of the sun did not offer a sufficiently reliable basis to firmly determine longer time sequences, the main units of time – the year, the month and the day – were decided on the basis of the motions of other heavenly bodies. The moon and its easily distinguishable cyclic phases of waxing and waning[133] were most frequently taken as indicators which were sufficiently stable to reckon the elapse of time after them.[134] Consequently, most of the calendars of the ancient Near Eastern civilizations had a lunar character.

In addition to this practical point for following a lunar calendar, in the Near Eastern cultures the moon was an object of religious adoration from times immemorial. From the context of our light-polluted world we can hardly imagine the impact that the moon had on an ancient mind and the

---

130. Engnell 1970: 190–91.
131. Segal 1963: 266.
132. Segal 1963: 266.
133. Ps. 104.19; Sir. 43.6–8. (6) He made the moon also, to serve in its season to mark the times and to be an everlasting sign. (7) From the moon comes the sign for feast days, a light that wanes when it has reached the full. (8) The month is named for the moon, increasing marvellously in its phases, an instrument of the hosts on high shining forth in the firmament of heaven.
134. Cohen 1993.

feeling of awe that probably seized an ancient observer while watching its constantly changing face. Numerous myths related to the moon and lunar deities almost tempt one to claim that, in fact, this primordial, divine nature of the moon and the deeply religious feeling that it generated[135] were the crucial reasons behind the preference for lunar calendars in ancient Near Eastern cultures. So much the more, because there are indications that, although hard to observe and define, the solar year and its phases were not completely unknown to the ancient peoples. In the case of the Egyptians, it is almost certain that they were familiar with it since at one stage of their history they tried to replace the lunar year of 354 days with the solar year of 365 days. In Mesopotamia and Israel, important religious festivals such as the Babylonian Akitu and the Israelite Passover and Tabernacles were concentrated at the time of the equinoxes, phenomena of the tropic year, which indicates that those two cultures also had knowledge of the phases of the sun and the solar year. However, what was the level of that knowledge, whether they were able to calculate the exact dates of these phenomena or whether they just knew their approximate times are questions that still await definite answers. According to M. Nilsson's broad research of time-reckoning among comparable cultures, it is more probable that they were aware of the equinoctial or solstitial seasons, but were not able to calculate the exact dates on which these solar phenomena occurred. Calculating the precise date of the equinoxes is particularly difficult and seldom undertaken. If the phases of the sun play any role in the calculation of time, the more frequent way of doing it is by observing the solstices.[136] There are indications that in addition to the equinoxes the Israelites were also familiar with the exact number of days in the solar year,[137] but this knowledge never crystallized into an official solar system of time-reckoning.

The lunar year, however, is approximately 11 days shorter than the solar, so, after several years of strictly following a calendar based on the phases of the moon, a drastic discrepancy occurs between the natural season of the year and that of the calendar. In order to correct this discrepancy, the lunar year was from time to time rectified. The Babylonians corrected their calendars by adding an intercalary month every two or three years. The decision whether the extra month was needed or not was based on empirical observation. If a natural cyclic

---

135.   One of the most frequent accusations of Yahweh regarding Israel's unfaithfulness is adoration of the sun, moon and the stars. Deut. 4.19; 17.3; 2 Kgs 23.5; Jer. 8.2.

136.   Nilsson 1920: 311.

137.   In Gen. 5.23 it is said that Enoch lived for 365 years. Also, the flood lasts from the 17th day of the second month till the 27th of the next year which is the lunar year of 354 days plus 11 days to equate it to the solar year. Gen. 7.11; 8.14.

event, such as harvest or flooding was out of step with the official calendar, an additional month was intercalated.[138]

The Israelites also used intercalation as a method to correct the lagging lunar year. However, according to Segal, the parameters by which the Israelites adapted the lunar year to fit the framework of the natural year were the two equinoctial points in the sun's annual course, or in other words the feasts of Passover and Tabernacles.[139] According to him, Passover and Tabernacles were celebrated on the dates of the vernal and autumnal equinox. Being aware, though, that nothing in the Bible or outside of it can substantiate his theory, he further claims that the method of intercalation was one of the most jealously kept secrets of the priesthood and that as such it did not find its way into the writings of the Bible, a book that holds no secrets since it was intended for the public.[140]

As we have said earlier, there is little doubt that the ancient Near Eastern cultures were aware of the existence of the equinoxes. The mere experience of alternating periods in which the days were progressively longer or shorter certainly taught them that there were points in the annual course of the sun when the length of the day and the night were equal. The equinoctial points were just two more in a series of other natural cycles through which life moved during the year. But it is hardly believable that the Israelites used the dates of the equinoxes as parameters to adjust the lunar year, as Segal suggests. As a matter of fact, even as late as the first century CE they used the same empirical method as the Babylonians, the simplicity of which would hardly qualify it for a jealously kept secret, as Segal claims. In a letter of Rabbi Gamaliel II from the first century CE to the diaspora Jews, he explains that he decided to add another thirty days to the year because the birds and the lambs were still weak and the grain was still not ripe.[141] If in the first century CE, the head of the Sanhedrin in the two decades before the destruction of the temple and certainly one of the most learned rabbis in that period used a very simple intercalation method based on expected occurrences in nature, it is quite improbable that the priests of the monarchic period were undertaking complex calculations of precise dates of the equinoxes in order to decide on the dates of Passover and Tabernacles and rectify the calendar. The point is whether they were actually capable of doing it given that even the Babylonians who were very experienced sky observers and

138. Cohen 1993: 5.

139. Segal 1963: 127.

140. 'That the equinox is not mentioned in the Bible – nor in Jewish documents before Philo – should cause no surprise. The Bible was intended for the public. It holds no secrets that the public should not know. And the secrets of the calendar – and among them the method of intercalation was most important – must have been guarded by the priesthood with jealous care.' Segal 1963: 127.

141. Finegan 1964: 43.

quite accomplished mathematicians used simplistic intercalation methods. However, what the mere fact that the lunar calendars were corrected demonstrates is that ancient calendars, including the Israelite, were closely bound to the cycles of nature, the vegetation processes and agriculture. As systems for reckoning the elapse of time, they were relevant only if the calendric months or periods coincided with the annual natural cyclic occurrences and seasons. If Segal's theory, that Passover was a festival dedicated to the national god Yahweh without any reference or relevance to the season in which it took place, is correct, one might rightfully ask what was, then, the purpose of adjusting the calendar at all? If the Israelites were interested only in the precise day of the vernal equinox in order to observe Passover and if the festival was meant to correspond only with that particular day, they could have followed a non-rectified lunar calendar, similar to the Islamic one in which the same months are in different natural seasons every year. It would not matter in which particular calendrical month it was celebrated as long as its observation was held on the day of the equinox. The fact that they rectified the calendar, however, points out that the calendar and its months and dates were relevant only if they corresponded with the natural seasons.

With respect to Passover, that means that the festival had to be observed during the month of Abib, the month whose name translates as 'the ears of corn',[142] clearly pointing to its association with an agriculturally relevant stage. Cohen actually claims that Abib is not a month designation, but an indication of the period (in the month *of Abib*[143]) when Passover should take place.[144] Perhaps this is the reason why Abib as a month name is not attested anywhere else outside the Bible in contrast to the other three non-Babylonian biblical months (Ziv,[145] Ethanim[146] and Bul[147]) which are found in Phoenician inscriptions.[148] Judging by the way the Abib is emphasized in the Bible, as the appointed season for Passover,[149] it is evident that the only possible time for the festival was during the month when the ears of barley were already formed and standing. The regressing lunar calendar had to be corrected in order

---

142.   De Vaux 1965: I, 183. According to Ginsberg it means 'milky ears of grain' (1982: 60). According to Harris, Abib refers to barley that is already ripe, but still soft (1980: 3).

143.   *Hodesh haabib* (month of ears of corn) as contrasted to *hodesh abib* (month 'ears of corn').

144.   Cohen 1993: 385.

145.   1 Kgs 6.1, 37.

146.   1 Kgs 8.2.

147.   1 Kgs 6.38.

148.   De Vaux 1965: I, 183.

149.   Exod. 23.15; 34.18; Deut. 16.1.

to synchronize the calendrical months with the real conditions on the fields because Passover was relevant for the oncoming season of harvest.

Segal also fails to notice (or chooses not to) the specific climatic conditions of Palestine during the vernal and the autumnal equinoctial months which are also months of seasonal climatic changes and corresponding vegetation processes. In Palestine those changes are experienced more dramatically than in regions with more temperate climates. The exchange of seasons is quick and intense and rather than four it is more appropriate to talk about two seasons, a hot, dry, summer and a cold, rainy, winter season. The routine usage of the words autumn and spring in the context of Palestine is somewhat inaccurate and misleading. The biblical frequent pairing of the two seasons[150] is in concordance with this climatic dichotomy of the year; summer being associated with the time of the harvest, winter with seed time.[151] The two months in which Passover and Tabernacles took place were indeed the months that expressed the equinoctial dichotomy of the tropic year, but they were also the months in which the beginnings of the harvest and the ploughing seasons were expected.

In view of its date, it is more likely that the observance of Passover was fixed for the night of the full moon[152] near the time of equinox. Given that the beginning of the month was calculated from the appearance of the new moon, the 14th day during one full lunation designated the night when the waxing cycle was completed. From Philo we know that it was around the time of the spring equinox, but the point is that his statement must not be taken literally in a sense that it happened on the date of the equinox. As a matter of fact, the date of the equinox and the date of the night of the full moon during the equinoctial month hardly ever coincide. In the past fifty years, for example, they coincided only three times, in 1962, 1989 and 2000.[153]

However, although Segal's theory about Passover's date being fixed to the spring equinox proved to be unsustainable, there is still the problem to be discussed of whether Passover was a kind of a calendric New Year festival, as both Segal and Engnell claim.

In the festal calendars of Exod. 23.15–16, 34.18–22, Deut. 16.1–16, Lev. 23.5–36 and the rituals in Num. 28.16–26, 29.1–12 and Ezek. 45.21–25, Passover is always mentioned as the first in a series of three festivals,[154]

---

150. Gen. 8.22; Ps. 74.17; Isa. 18.6; Amos 3.15.

151. Gen. 8.22: While the earth remains, seedtime and harvest, cold and heat, summer and winter, day and night, shall not cease. Jer. 8.20: The harvest is past, the summer is ended, and we are not saved.

152. Exod. 12.18; Lev. 23.5; Num. 9.3; 28.16; Ezek. 45.21.

153. I found these data on the internet. 'Trend Analysis of Full Moon and Vernal Equinoxes' by C. Marwardt. http://cow.physics.wisc.edu/~craigm/moonvern/

154. Ezek. 45.21–25 omits the Feast of Weeks.

which suggests that it opened the cycle of the three pilgrimage feasts and stood in the first month of the religious calendar. The month is either determined as Abib[155] or the first month.[156] The Feast of Tabernacles, which took place six months after Passover, in the seventh month,[157] rounded off and closed the cultic cycle. In many of its traits it was similar to Passover: they both lasted seven days and were marked by holy convocations in the shrine; the time and the date of their observance coincided with the nights of the full moon in the months of the spring and autumn equinox, the months which divided the year into a dry and a rainy season, harvest time and ploughing time. Passover took place at the beginning of the summer season, when, after the long winter pause, the barley was ripe and ready or almost ready to be harvested. The Feast of Tabernacles was observed at the end of the summer season and at the beginning of the rainy season, in the month of Ethanim, the month in which only the perennial streams were still flowing,[158] when the fruit harvest and the vintage were over.

While the position of Passover with regard to the beginning of the year in the religious calendar is quite clear and is a matter of considerable agreement among scholars,[159] the question of its position in the secular year is quite controversial. Generally, the main division refers to whether the month of Passover or the month of Tabernacles represents the beginning of the secular year. The arguments in support of Ethanim, the autumn month, as the first month in the secular year and thus indirectly for Tabernacles as the New Year feast, are usually based on the phrases such as 'going out' of the year (literal translation of Exod. 23.16) and 'the return' of the year (literal translation of 1 Chron. 20.1 and 1 Kgs 20.22, 26) that are in the Old Testament used in connection with Tabernacles.[160] However, scholars who favour a spring beginning to the year point to Lev. 23.5, Num. 28.16 and Ezek. 45.21 where the month of Passover is designated as the first month.

Some scholars explain this contradiction of having two first months in a single natural year as a result of the shift that moved the beginning of the year from autumn to spring, holding that originally Tabernacles was the New Year feast.[161] Others, like Segal, argue that from early times the beginning of the year of the Israelites was in spring and that Passover was the New Year feast.[162] Pedersen, on the other hand, allows that both

155. Exod. 23.15; 34.18, 25; Deut. 16.1.
156. Lev. 23.5; Num. 28.16; Ezek. 45.21.
157. Lev. 23.34.
158. De Vaux 1965: I, 183.
159. De Vaux 1965: II, 503; Pedersen 1959: 445; Wellhausen 1885: 85.
160. De Vaux 1965: I, 190; Gray 1925: 30;. De Moor 1972: I, 12.
161. Gray 1925: 300; Van Goudoever 1961: 36; Langdon 1933: 97; De Moor 1972: I, 12.
162. Segal 1963: 114.

festivals were in some respect New Year feasts.[163] He points out that the phrases such as 'going out' and the 'return' of the year do not refer to a calendar year of 12 months,[164] but to the summer season or the harvest season which dies out at the time of the fruit harvest in order to reappear or revive at the time of the barley harvest in spring.[165] Clines also suggests that the phrases could be an indication of a change in the course of the seasonal year rather than definite points in a calendar.[166] Still others argue that those phrases might refer to equinoctial time points.[167] However, as far as our discussion is concerned and the possibility that Passover was a New Year festival of the secular calendar, this variety of opinions only indicates that we cannot draw any reliable conclusions on the basis of the phraseology of the Old Testament.

The Israelite natural year, as already mentioned, was divided into two seasons, winter and summer, the seed time and the time of the harvest. It is quite possible that originally both festivals were some kind of New Year feasts which, however, did not mark the beginning of a 12-month year, but the beginning or respectively the end of the two natural seasons, thus causing a confusion among modern minds who take for granted that the expression 'year' must invariably comprise all seasons of the natural year or that a year must have only one beginning. Depending on the phenomenon that one wants to chronologically follow or observe in a fixed period of time, there can be many diverse beginnings or 'New Years' in the course of a single calendar year and those beginnings do not necessarily correspond with the official beginning of the calendric year. The Rabbis, for example, reckoned there were four different beginnings to the year: 'in Nisan, the New Year for kings and for festivals; in Elul, the New Year for the tithe on cattle; in Tishri, the New Year for years, the sabbatical year and the Jubilee year; in Shebat, the New Year for the tithe on trees'.[168] Roland de Vaux argues that these four beginnings are a result of the Rabbis' lack of distinguishing between the relative ages of texts in the Old Testament.[169] However, De Vaux overlooks that we, like the Rabbis, also have diverse beginnings in one year for different contexts of life: for the fiscal year, for the academic year, for the year itself, and so on.

---

163. Pedersen 1959: 444–46. Pedersen maintains that Passover as a vernal beginning of the year was of Israelite origin, while the autumnal beginning of the year belonged to the Canaanite tradition.

164. According to Nilsson, the *pars pro toto* method of time-reckoning which takes one season to designate the whole year is a very common way of calculating the time among ancient people. Nilsson 1920: 358.

165. Pedersen 1959: 444–45.

166. Clines 1998: 378.

167. Cohen 1993: 6.

168. The Mishnah, *Rosh Hashanah* 1.1. Neusner 1988: 299.

169. De Vaux 1965: I, 193.

This rabbinical tradition, on the other hand, seems to indirectly support the theories that postulate that both Passover and Tabernacles were some kind of New Year festivals, though each for a different season of the natural year or for different things; Passover for the harvest and the sacral year, while Tabernacles would have the role of inaugurating the seedtime season and the secular year. The closeness of Tabernacles and the much later introduced Rosh Hashanah, the New Year, also speaks in favour of this way of reasoning. However, what seems certain is that none of them had the character of an official calendar New Year festival, in which case the date for their observance would have probably been the 1st of Nisan or the 1st of Tishri.[170]

This mystifying lack of a cyclic time climax of the Israelite calendar year at one definite point and its multiplication into two time points without priority – a feature that confuses scholars who routinely think in terms of later formalized, calendrical New Year feasts – is actually not restricted to the region of Palestine. The famous Mesopotamian Akitu in Babylon was celebrated once a year, in spring, but in its earliest Sumerian version in Ur, Nippur, Uruk and Adab it was celebrated twice.[171] The most frequently mentioned months are the first and the seventh, which stood at the beginning of each half of the year. The majority of scholars regard Akitu as primarily a New Year festival, the function of which did not relate to either the climatic or vegetation processes,[172] while some find that its main feature was the death and the resurrection of the fertility god, which represented the change in the natural seasons.[173] Akitu had a very lengthy and complex development and it is very hard to decide on its function because it certainly changed over the millennia in which it was celebrated. That at least in some of its versions Akitu occurred in relation to the natural seasons is best demonstrated by Sumerian documents, in which the celebration in the first month is called 'the a-ki-ti festival of the harvesting' while the one in the seventh month was 'the a-ki-ti of the seeding'.[174]

On the other hand, the lack of a real New Year feast among the Israelites that would mark a beginning of a calendar year of 12 months should not surprise us. The pre-Yahwistic Israelite religion had a very concrete character and was essentially connected to the cycles of nature. An abstract beginning of an abstract year without any reference to the very concrete nature of things such as climate and agriculture, on which the survival of the community depended, did not have any meaning or

170.   De Vaux 1965: II, 502.
171.   Cohen 1993: 401; James 1962: 140; Pedersen 1959: 747; Pallis 1926: 26.
172.   Segal 1963: 122–23; De Vaux 1965: II, 508; Pedersen 1959: 747.
173.   Pallis 1926: 249.
174.   Cohen 1993: 406.

significance. The two festivals, Passover and Tabernacles, both stood at the beginning and at the end of two natural seasons and in that respect there was no preference or priority between them given that both were of equal importance for the well-being of the people.

Conclusions

The most important conclusion in light of the previous discussion is that Passover carries as a single festival across various legislative texts. That conclusion dismisses the almost habitually assumed and most often suggested development, the fusion between two independent feasts, strongly indicating instead that Yahwistic interventions mostly focused on the reinterpretation of the purpose and the meaning of the festival without many changes in its ritual structure and organization. The resolution as to whether there is any ground on which it is possible to claim that Passover was formed by amalgamation was of major importance since now we can claim that there is an internal coherence between the ritual during the first night and the rest of the festival, regardless of how incomprehensible at the moment the particular function of the former appears in the overall structure of Passover. Given that three of the festival's individual rituals that we know about – Passover sacrifice, the sheaf and unleavened bread – can now be regarded as parts of one whole makes it possible that their symbolic references correspond as well and justifies an attempt of inclusive interpretation of the symbolic system of the festival.

The only real development in its ritual organization that could be detected from the texts referred to the location of the performance of the first-day ceremonies. In contrast to many theories in which centralization features as the cause of the alleged merger, in our analysis it has proved to be the cause of an opposite movement. The restriction of only the opening day to the central shrine resulted in a disturbance of the festival's spatial organization and coherence, which most likely led to the multiplicity of its names: Passover, Unleavened Bread and Sheaf. The texts were also tested against other frequently used arguments in favour of the theory about Passover's dual origin. The discussion of the likelihood that the Exodus legislation reflects the familial nature of the Passover sacrifice revealed that this specific ritual actually had a group character while its authentic place of performance was the temple. The investigation of the argument that the Passover sacrifice was of pastoral origin in contrast to unleavened bread, which is alleged to typify the agricultural customs, uncovered Passover's connection with the sphere of fertility.

The discussion threw light on other important features of Passover such as that it was probably held in more than one location before the centralization; that the providers of animals for the ritual on the first day of the festival were not restricted to families, but included also the priests and the royal family; that the handling of the sacrificial animals, both the killing and manipulation of the blood, was done mainly by priests; and finally that the collective eating of the animal occurred within the enclosure of the temple.

With respect to its purpose before the Yahwistic transformation, the time of its performance suggests that Passover was not a calendrical, but a seasonal festival most probably associated with the beginning of the grain harvest and the related cycle of vegetation processes and climatic changes. The date of the opening ceremonies of the festival was most probably fixed for the night of the full moon during the month of the vernal equinox. Given the similarities that exist between Passover and Tabernacles in terms of their timing and duration, Passover (and Tabernacles) appears more as a semi-annual rather than an annual event.

Overall, the picture of Passover painted by the legislative texts is that of a typical seasonal temple festival with a variety of elaborate sacrifices and rites that involved the participation of the priests, the royal family and the public as well. The texts preserve four main rituals: the ritual of eating the flesh of the sacrificial animal on the first night; the cutting and waving of the first sheaf of barley on the second night; the gathering on its seventh day; and, finally, the consumption of unleavened bread that was upheld from the opening to the closing day. The observance of the first two rituals is connected with a temple, while all four involved the participation of the community. Two of them were performed at night. The sacrificial animal of the first night was killed in the evening and eaten during the night. Although not stated in the biblical texts, the Mishnah preserves the detail that the first sheaf of barley that was offered during Passover was also cut during the night.[175] Another characteristic of the festival was the removal and avoidance of leaven which found its ritual expression in the eating of the unleavened bread.

The aforementioned rites and ritual elements are only pieces of the festival, and the incompleteness of the preserved picture does not allow a definite conclusion regarding the festival's pre-commemorative function to be reached. It was undoubtedly connected with the fertility cult and the beginning of the harvest season, but in which particular way it related to them cannot be surmised from the legislative texts of the Bible. On the other hand, a full understanding of that pre-commemorative function is crucial if we are to attempt an interpretation of Passover's symbolism, since the employment and the arrangement of its individual ritual elements, given that Yahwism did not unnecessarily intervene in that respect, is in relation and reference to that function. In order to reveal and understand the essence of Passover before it was transformed into a

---

175. The Mishnah, *Menaḥot* 10.1–5. Neusner 1988: 753–54.

commemorative festival, we will have to turn to historical accounts in which particular celebrations of Passover are mentioned and see whether the mentioning of those individual observances as part of wider narratives has any symbolic capacity that can be taken as a reflection of Passover's pre-commemorative function.

PART III

Chapter 3

SYMBOLISM OF PASSOVER

3.1. *Symbolism of Passover in Biblical Narratives*

The historical narratives of the Old Testament are most often read and researched for the eventual facts they might provide about the times and the events they describe, the protagonists of those events, and so on. However, as was said earlier, we shall treat the reports relating to individual Passover celebrations as basically ahistorical, meaning that in terms of the reported events, including Passover events, they do not reflect any reality. Instead, the accounts will be taken as symbolic stories that communicate implicit messages about Passover, whose meaning can be understood only if we penetrate beyond the level of the clearly perceptible and intentional Yahwistic ideology.

In the sacred history of the Israelites almost every important stage includes a Passover celebration. The introduction of each particular stage most often takes a form of an event and the symbolic references of the festival are in relation to those events. Keeping in mind Leach's suggestion that religious texts contain mysteries that are still decodable from the text itself,[1] we might conclude that our task is to consider the role of these celebrations within the wider context of the narratives and whether that role can be seen as symbolic.

So what then are the larger narrative structures within which individual Passover celebrations are mentioned?

The first Passover happens in Egypt on the night before the Israelites depart and is closely connected to the tenth plague that kills the Egyptian firstborn.[2]

The Passover on Sinai takes place after all the laws of Yahweh are declared and the Tabernacle finished.[3] One can argue that the Sinai celebration does not constitute an event since it is a part of the regulations on second Passover. However, although the rules on the second Passover are dominant, they are nevertheless presented within the context of a

---

1. Leach and Aycock 1983: 3.
2. Exod. 12.
3. Num. 9.4–6.

certain story. The preparations for the Passover actually start on the first day after Moses finished setting up the Tabernacle. Every following day is separately accounted for, with elaborate descriptions of offerings for the altar, brought by twelve tribal leaders. On the thirteenth day, Levites are consecrated as a substitution for sparing the Israelite firstborn in Egypt and, just after that, on the fourteenth day, comes the celebration of Passover, as the event that crowns the whole of the preceding ceremonial presentation of offerings. It is evident from the general framework of the narrative that the celebration of Passover is its integral part and that it certainly has a definite purpose within that narrative. That purpose, on the other hand, is certainly not to be a convenient introduction for the regulations on second Passover. In fact, within the context, the regulations seem to be secondary, being very awkwardly interpolated with an apparent discrepancy between the question asked by the people and the answer Moses gives them.[4]

After the Passover in Sinai comes the first Passover in Canaan,[5] following the miraculous crossing of the Jordan (an obvious duplication of the crossing of the Sea of Reeds), and the arrival of the Israelites on the territory of the 'promized land'.

In the narratives about the construction of the temple, the situation is somewhat more complicated than in other narratives, since Passover is mentioned along with other cultic ceremonies as a conclusion to the works on the temple and not as a real celebration.[6] The first festival that is described to have been organized by Solomon in the newly built temple is that of Tabernacles. However, as we have seen in one of the previous chapters, Passover and Tabernacles were very similar and there are strong indications that they were doublet festivals. Why Tabernacles in the case of the story regarding the building of the temple is mentioned instead of Passover will be clear later.[7] For the time being, it will suffice to say that because of their strong organizational resemblance we shall consider the role of Tabernacles in this narrative to be the same as Passover's in other stories.

Hezekiah's Passover comes after the temple has been re-sanctified and the long period of kings who worshipped other gods.[8]

---

4. Num. 9.6–11. Moses's answer explains the particular cases in which a second Passover is allowed (being unclean, on a journey), but that actually does not clarify the original question: why are those who are unclean through touching a dead body prevented from keeping it in its right time?

5. Josh. 5.10–12.

6. 1 Kgs 9.25; 2 Chron. 8.12–13.

7. See section 3.3.4, 'The Sacrificial Animal'.

8. 2 Chron. 30.

Josiah's Passover follows the religious purge that eradicated pagan idols, sacred places and priests.[9]

Finally, there is the Passover celebration held after the people returned from the exile and the temple was rebuilt.[10]

In all these narratives, the Passover celebration is described differently. In the book of Exodus it is presented as a rite whose main purpose is to enable Yahweh to recognize the homes of the Israelites and pass over them in his deadly mission. The focus is on the handling of blood that is poured in the basin and sprinkled onto the houses with a bunch of hyssop. The inhabitants of the house are to remain in the house for the rest of the night. There is no mention of the unleavened bread.

The Passover held immediately after entering Canaan presents a completely different picture. Men must be circumcized before they are allowed to observe the festival. The celebration is held on the evening of the 14th, in a special place. The next morning unleavened cakes and parched grain are eaten. Manna ceases.

The Bible does not give any details about the Passover kept in Sinai except that it is kept on the 14th day of the first month in the evening. People who were at the time of its observance in touch with dead bodies are banned from the festival.

Solomon's festival is held in the newly built temple with many sacrifices. However, it should be mentioned that the most prominent role in officiating the festival ceremonies belongs to the king.[11]

Hezekiah's and Josiah's Passovers are elaborately described. The descriptions include details about the holy assembly, royal contribution of Passover lambs, killing of the sacrificial victims, sprinkling of blood, eating of unleavened bread, singing and ritual sanctification. In both accounts, the accent is on purity and the Levites are assigned the task of killing the sacrificial animals. In the account of Josiah's Passover, observance of the Feast of the Unleavened Bread is mentioned separately, while Hezekiah's Passover takes place in the second month and instead of seven it is kept for 14 days.

In the Passover of the returned exiles, the accent is also on purity and, again, the Levites are the ones who kill the Passover lamb on behalf of the rest of the community. The Feast of the Unleavened Bread is kept for seven days.

The first impression one gets from reading all the narrated events and Passover descriptions is that there is not a single element that can be identified as common to all of them. Some of the events seem to refer to the history of the cult, such as the law declaration on Sinai, the building of the

9. 2 Kgs 21–23; 2 Chron. 35.1–19.
10. Ezra 6.19–22.
11. 1 Kgs 8.62–65.

temple and the religious reforms of Josiah and Hezekiah. Others, such as the exodus, entering into Canaan and the return from exile, seem to relate the mundane history of the Israelites. Moreover, the descriptions of Passover vary significantly from occasion to occasion and it is evident that in some cases the final compilers either overemphasized some of its features or even designed new ones in an effort to achieve congruity with the nature of the alleged historical circumstances in which the celebrations took place.

However, all these differences are differences of detail and, as the critics of the positivistic method would remark, as long as we are interested in trees we will not be able to see the forest. When stripped of the variations introduced by the intention of the authors to have them as histories, these stories actually reveal a very consistent general structure that in each individual case repeats the same basic elements. In short, they all follow the same organizational and structural pattern.

The first of the structural elements that appears as a constant is certainly the mere mentioning of Passover as part of the narrated events. Its inclusion cannot be accidental because if the same thing is repeated more than once (in our case seven times) then it ceases to be accidental and becomes a pattern, otherwise it would not reappear. What it indicates is that Passover itself, that is its mentioning, serves as a common designator that in some specific sense separates these particular legends from other events in the sacred history of the Israelites. That, on the other hand, makes it possible to assume that the meaning of Passover, as it is included in the narratives, goes beyond the plane of the clearly perceptible and that it is not limited to the theologically declared one, honouring of Yahweh and remembering the flight from Egypt. On closer inspection, it becomes clear that commemoration is not the only reason for incorporating the celebrations into these tales because that particular meaning only partially corresponds with the described circumstances of each one of the mentioned occasions. If it is perhaps warranted and self-evident in the case of Joshua's entry into Canaan as the fulfilment of Yahweh's promise given on the occasion of exodus that he will give them land or for similar reasons in the case of the returned exiles, it is much less warranted in other situations in which we come across Passover celebrations. One might ask what was the intention behind the inclusion of a festival remembering exodus into events such as the giving of the law on Sinai or Hezekiah's sanctification of the temple or Josiah's religious purge? What was the unifying idea between these events and Passover that the author consciously or unconsciously projected by asserting the festival's observance?

What appears when we move our attention from the obvious climax in these stories to the way they are structured, is that Passover plays the role of an intermediary element between two clearly defined stages in the history of the Israelites. In exodus, it concludes the period in which they were slaves and introduces the period of freedom. On Sinai, it comes after all the laws of Yahweh are declared and the Tabernacle is erected, thus starting the new life governed by the ordinances of the covenant with the god of the Israelites. The Passover in Canaan closes the period of destitution during the wandering in the wilderness and inaugurates the abundance of the new homeland. Solomon's festival completes the period of tabernacle as Yahweh's dwelling place and begins the era of the temple. Both Hezekiah's and Josiah's Passovers end periods of faithlessness and come as a sign that the covenant with Yahweh and his rule are re-established. Passover in Ezra closes the exile and introduces the new life in Israel. It is more than clear that these conditions mediated by Passover are in each case fundamentally different, and that they stand in an antithetical correlation. Thus we have the opposites 'death/life' and their derivatives 'slavery/freedom' (exodus), 'wanting/abundance' (Canaan), 'non-existence of law/establishment of law' (Sinai), 'temporary sanctuary/permanent sanctuary' (Solomon), 'defilement/purification' (Hezekiah), 'worship of many/worship of one' (Josiah), and finally 'exile/homeland' (return from exile).

Such a structure, which consists of binary oppositions, is most often found in myths.[12] Genesis, which is traditionally regarded as the part of the Bible which contains the majority of mythological material, abounds in explicit examples. God creates heaven and earth,[13] day and night,[14] dry land and seas.[15] Cain and Abel are respectively farmer and shepherd.[16] When the flood is over, making a vow that he will never again send another flood, God says that while the earth remains, seedtime and harvest, cold and heat, summer and winter, day and night, shall not cease.[17] Although not as explicitly as the examples from Genesis, biblical stories that incorporate celebrations of Passover into their plot lines conform to the same pattern of ordering the world. Having a mythic structure, on the other hand, does not necessarily relegate these stories into the sphere of mythology and does not automatically mean that they do not have anything to do with historical truth. One may argue that if not in their totality then at least in some of their details they are neither mythical nor ideological projections, but historical facts, such as the existence of Josiah for example, and that treating them as myths would be wrong. However, such an argument would be relevant if the biblical text were historiography in the sense that we usually ascribe to it: a discipline that conforms to the modern way of rationalizing events in history. The

12. Levi-Strauss 1955.
13. Gen. 1.1.
14. Gen. 1.5.
15. Gen. 1.10.
16. Gen. 4.2.
17. Gen. 8.22.

point is that what we are dealing with in the biblical text is some kind of national historiography, but that historiography is of the kind that still does not make a clear distinction between the mythical and the real.[18] It both transforms mythological figures and events into historical ones and assigns mythological qualities to historical figures and events.[19] Such a national history where the mythical and the real are so closely intertwined demonstrates that, in matters of rationalizing events, the Bible still pertains to the mythological pattern of thinking. The events incorporating Passover celebrations and presented as historical were moulded according to that pattern and show a structure proper to myths, because their significance for the history and the associated, inseparable history of Yahweh was felt to be of mythological proportions. They are, in Levi-Strauss's parlance, the mythemes on the mythological axis that begins with exodus and ends with the return from exile. The exodus initiates a chain of events along that axis, events that on the level of phenomenal appearances seem different but basically deal with reinforcing the three quintessential elements of the Yahwistic ideology: the land claim, the law and the temple. The land claim is established by Joshua's crossing of the Jordan. The law and the temple are each twice affirmed. The law is declared on Sinai and re-declared by Josiah after he finds the long-lost book of law. Solomon builds the temple, but it becomes desecrated and dysfunctional under Ahaz. Hezekiah cleanses it and re-opens it. The exile effectively reverses all of these achievements and is another period of symbolical wandering through the wilderness without law, land and temple. The return from the exile is the convergence point in which all three elements find their re-actualization. Ezra re-establishes claim to the land, brings the law and rebuilds the temple.

In each of these mythemes that deal with the establishment or re-establishment of the core elements of Yahwistic theology we find Passover functioning as an intermediary between opposed conditions. According to Leach, exactly this 'middle ground' between binary oppositions is 'typically the focus of all taboo and ritual observance'.[20] In myths, this category is usually represented by contradictory beings who possess qualities of both antipodes, such as virgin mothers or dying gods. In biblical stories where Passover is mentioned, there is not a single reference to any such being, unless we take 'the destroyer' from Exodus as being contradictory since its involvement means both death and life, death for the Egyptians, and indirectly, by passing over marked houses, life and freedom for the Israelites. However, regardless of whether 'the destroyer' can be taken as a relic from the original myth or not, it is evident from the

---

18.   Johnstone 1990: 31–36.
19.   Goldziher 1967: 250–58; Fishbane 1985: 356–57.
20.   Leach 1969: 11.

general structural pattern of biblical stories, in which its observance is asserted, that Passover's role is to mediate, to cover some kind of a 'middle ground' between alleged events in the history of the relationship between the Israelites and their god.

In the context of narratives, that role of mediation entails several functions. It serves to differentiate and separate the conditions, thus stressing their contrasting qualities, then to ease the transition from one to another stage and, finally, to advance the new condition. However, the distribution among these functions is not even, and sometimes there is more stress on separation, sometimes on the transition and sometimes on the new conditions. In the Passover in Egypt the accent is obviously on separation (marking of the houses). In the Passovers of Hezekiah and Josiah the more prominent part is allocated to its transitional function (both stress the length of the festival with Hezekiah's Passover even celebrated for two weeks, which diverges from the usual practice), and advancement of the new condition (both are especially joyful celebrations), while the focus in the first Passover in Canaan is on the advancement of the new conditions (eating of the produce of the new land).

Such manifold yet dialectically interrelated functions are usually associated with various types of rites of passage.[21] Their main purpose, according to Arnold van Gennep, is to enable the passage 'from one defined condition to another that is equally well defined'.[22] As we have seen, the same purpose is allocated to Passover in each of our stories. However, it is never given in an explicit form. Its message of mediation is transmitted only implicitly, and Passover in these tales is not a reality, but a symbol that the opposed conditions are properly dealt with.

This combination, where, on the one hand, we have narratives that despite being presented as historical happenings maintain a mythical structure and, on the other hand, a festival the purpose of which is at an historical level obscure but is almost self-evident at the level of the mythical, undoubtedly points out that inclusion of Passover as part of these stories also derives from the mythical pattern of understanding the world. Within that cultural pattern, in times when the destiny of the Israelites was perceived to depend not just on historical events but on mythological events as well, Passover was obviously a rite of passage that signified a change of conditions and that is the function that it symbolically performs in the narratives.

Rites of passage, on the other hand, regardless of the kind of turning point they negotiate, are not observed only in order to mark the change, but because they are themselves regarded as being the agent that induces

21. Van Gennep 1960: 11.
22. Van Gennep 1960: 3.

and actualizes the change in question.[23] It is important to emphasize that the character of Passover goes beyond mere performance, because not all festivals have transformative powers. The ones whose main function is commemoration, a function that the Bible assigns to Passover as well, only mark dates of important events and do not initiate or bring any change. There is little doubt that in pre-Yahwistic times this transformative festival was for the Israelites extremely significant and relevant otherwise it would not be mentioned as part of the events that deal with the development of the main tenets of the Yahwistic theology. It could have been the rite of passage *par excellence*, the ultimate rite of passage, parallel to the Babylonian Akitu or other important seasonal rites of passage such as the Egyptian Osirian festivals or the Greek Eleusinian mysteries. Being clear that Passover also belongs to this category of transformative festivals is crucial for our pending discussion of the symbolism of its individual aspects because only from this perspective can that symbolism be properly understood and interpreted.

There is another conclusion that can be drawn from these stories about Passover and its symbolic function as a rite of passage. The new condition that is initiated by Passover is never represented as a qualitatively indifferent change in a sense that it is just another development in the history of the Israelites. From the perspective of the Yahwistic system of values, Passover always means promotion of those values and the new condition is always an improvement of the one that preceded it. Passover always means betterment. Such definitely determined quality of the change symbolically initiated in these narratives by Passover is an indication that it had the same positive meaning even before its function was changed from a rite of passage to a commemoration. One of the tasks in the next chapters will be to see in which particular way Passover's individual elements such as the time organization and ritual acts reflect this meaning of positive change.

3.2. *Time Symbolism*

In discussing the time symbolism of Passover we shall deal with the two aspects of its time organization. First we shall consider its general time, that is the meaning of the season in which it takes place and the symbolic references of Passover pertaining to that season. After that we shall turn to the symbolic references of the time organization of its rituals, namely the eating of the sacrificial animal and the offering of sheaf.

---

23.   Grimes 2000: 6–7.

3.2.1. *The Season*

There are three elements in Passover's general time design that we directly or indirectly know about and whose meaning we shall discuss in order to establish the symbolism of Passover with respect to the season in which it takes place. Two of them, 'the first month' and 'the month of Abib' are given in the Bible,[24] while from Philo we learn that the month in question was the month of the vernal equinox.[25] The most unproblematic one to start the discussion with is Philo's determination since it precludes doubts regarding its meaning, which might arise if we start with the ones from the Bible. Philo's determinant provides the reality context to which we can tie the biblical expressions.

Being celebrated during the month of the vernal equinox is an indication that Passover had solar associations, given that equinoxes and solstices are phenomena related to the sun's annual course. None of the sun-related references has openly reached us through the biblical texts, but there is a solid body of evidence, both from biblical and non-biblical sources, which testifies that the solar cult had its followers in Palestine from an early stage. The Bible preserves toponyms such as Beth Shemesh,[26] En Shemesh[27] and Ir Shemesh.[28] Yahweh accuses and warns the Israelites against adoring the sun, the moon and the stars.[29] Before celebrating Passover in Jerusalem, Josiah removes from the temple the horses and the carriage dedicated to the sun and the priests who burn incense to the sun, the moon and the constellations.[30] Ezekiel witnesses men who, turned towards the east, worship the rising sun.[31] Yahweh is also portrayed as the sun. Psalm 89.12 openly declares: 'For the Lord God is the sun and shield'. Habakkuk 3.4 describes the brightness of Yahweh as the light from whose hands rays flash, a description which is very reminiscent of the Egyptian representation of sun rays as hands holding the sign of life. However, in contrast to the Egyptian representation where the sun is a symbol of life, in Habakkuk Yahweh in his solar aspect is a symbol of destruction.[32] Finally, two of the three seasonal festivals were

---

24. 'The first month' appears in Exod. 12.2, 8; Lev. 23.5; Num. 9.5; 28.16; 33.3; 2 Chron. 35.1; Ezek. 45.21. 'Abib' appears in Exod. 13.4; 23.15; 34.18; Deut. 16.1.

25. Philo, *Speci. Leg.* II, 151.

26. Josh. 15.10; 21.16.

27. Josh. 15.7; 18.17.

28. Josh. 19.41.

29. Deut. 4.19; 17.3.

30. 2 Kgs 23.11.

31. Ezek. 8.16.

32. It is possible to also see Yahweh from Habakkuk as the rain god with its typical attributes of thunder and lighting, but involvement of the carriage in which Yahweh rides and waters that tremble before his might as well as the havoc he wreaks, the withering vineyards, etc., indicate that Yahweh appears here as a solar divinity. The idea that the sun rides in a carriage across the sky was not unknown to the Israelites as 2 Kgs 23.11 testifies.

performed at the time of the vernal and the autumn equinox. In some form and among certain groups this adoration of the sun continued well into Roman times when Josephus Flavius wrote that the Essenes, turned towards east, recited ancestral prayers until dawn, as if they prayed for the sun to rise.[33]

The aforementioned examples quite significantly intimate that the sun as a force in its own right played a much more important role in the religious life of Palestine then it is possible to surmise from the Bible where Yahweh absorbed its major attributes. They are perhaps also an indication that before it was changed into a remembrance festival, Passover also had strong connections with the sun. Since, for the time being, we have no other indications of their nature we have to limit our investigation to the symbolism of the sun in its spring equinoctial aspect.

According to T. Gaster, who in many details discusses the nature of periodic festivals in the ancient Near East, connection with the equinoxes or the solstices is one of the main ingredients of seasonal festivals. Without actually discussing the particular meaning that the sun can have in each of the festivals quoted as examples, he explains that: 'The reason for this association is not hard to fathom: the re-emergence of the sun, especially in spring was an obvious date to reckon the renewal of the world's vitality; ... Similarly, the decline of the sun was a natural occasion from which to date the eclipse of such vitality.'[34] However, although the sun very often symbolizes decline and renewal of vitality, Gaster's understanding of the nature of the connection between the sun's phases and a wide spectre of seasonal festivals is extremely one-directional and based on the generalization that the sun invariably symbolizes life. The symbolism of the sun, however, is as polyvalent as its reality is varied and can have both negative and positive connotations. It can certainly mean life, but it can also mean death. Which distinctive meaning the sun has in any given ritual situation depends on a variety of factors, such as the geographical region, the idiosyncrasies of the terrain and the climate, the time of the year, the nature of the deity to whom the ritual refers, the aim of the rites themselves, and so on. Only when the sun is considered in relation to these other factors, can its meaning be decided. It can hardly be imagined that in Mesopotamia, for example, the connection between the sun and the rites of weeping for Tammuz, which took place around the summer solstice, was due to the perception that the sun's decline somehow mirrored the death of the god. Tammuz was a vegetation deity and considering the idiosyncratic geographical conditions of Mesopotamia it is hardly believable that the sun of the summer solstice in connection with vegetation had benevolent connotations. The sun of the summer solstice is

33.   Josephus, *The Jewish War* II, 128.
34.   Gaster 1975: 48.

in its climax and can easily represent its ominous, deadly side. Its implication in the death of Tammuz is more likely to have been in this negative aspect, as a force that actively contributes to the god's death rather than a force that represents the god himself.[35]

A similar criticism can be directed towards the explanation that the vernal equinox represents an obvious date for reckoning the renewed vitality of the world because of the sun's alleged re-emergence at this time of the year. Expressions such as 're-emerging', 'reawaking', 'reviving' and similar can be applied to much of the natural world in spring, but the big question is whether the same can be done in the case of the sun and in particular the sun in its equinoctial aspect. The time from which the sun is regaining its strength or regenerating is more likely to be associated with the winter solstice, the time of the year when the presence of the sun in the sky reaches its shortest period and following which the sun is again in an ascending phase. On winter solstice, the Romans very appropriately celebrated the festival of the *Sol Invictus*, the invincible sun, which Christianity took over and reinterpreted as Jesus' date of birth, a rendering that still contains the idea that the sun is born or re-born or re-emerging at the winter solstice. The successive increase of lighted candles during Hanukah, the Jewish festival introduced during Roman times, which also takes place around winter solstice, obviously reflects a similar understanding of the relation between the time of the year and the sun.

Gaster's imprecise interpretations stem mainly from his disregard of the fact that there are crucial differences between the sun in its spring, summer, winter or autumn aspect, and that establishing the true nature of associations that refer to these particular moments in the sun's annual course requires a more circumscribed perspective than the one of the clichéd 'sun is a symbol of life'. We can be sure that the ancient people, whose lives and daily activities were very much dependent on the rhythms of nature, were acutely aware of the sun's cycles and that the symbolic role of the sun within the symbolism of seasonal festivals reflects those differences.

Depending on the geographical region, the four distinctive points in the sun's annual course, the two solstices and the two equinoxes, can be quite conspicuous indicators of the changes in the natural seasons and respective vegetation processes, but the primary way in which they manifest is actually through the length of daylight. Among them the two equinoxes mark the alternating six-month cycles in which light or darkness, day or night prevail in duration. An association with the months in which the change between these two cycles takes place primarily involves the symbolic references of the sun as the force that brings light. In

---

35. Strangely enough, in discussing the conspicuous timing of seasonal rites Gaster claims that Tammuz rites were held in the month of the spring solstice (*sic*) and that Pentecost (Weeks) took place in the month of the spring equinox (*sic*). Gaster 1975: 47.

the Bible Yahweh is the one who governs over it;[36] however, there is little doubt that before Yahweh achieved the status of *primum mobile*, the sun was a power in its own right and was responsible for the duration of the day. Psalm 104.19 in which the sun is said to know the time of its own setting, although only indirectly, still preserves this idea.

Passover's solar associations, at least what we know about them, are therefore not with the sun in its general aspect, but with the sun as the light-bringing force. Being observed during the month of the vernal equinox indicates that it was a festival that inaugurated the bright half of the year, the half during which the length of the day dominated over that of the night. Philo confirms that light was the dominant aspect of the sun at Passover. He writes:

> The feast begins at the middle of the month, on the fifteenth of the month, when the moon is full, a day purposefully chosen because then there is no darkness, but everything is continuously lighted up as the sun shines from morning to evening and the moon from evening to morning and while the stars give place to each other no shadow is cast upon their brightness.[37]

The Bible also preserves a trace of this connection between Passover and the vernal sun in its light-bringing aspect. In a passage in Isa. 30.19–33 the prophet declares that Yahweh has not forgotten his people and that a time will come when they will be saved from oppression. The description of that time, in particular because Isaiah also mentions a feast, is, however, so suggestive of the time of Passover that it actually makes it possible to assume that this festival was the source that inspired the prophet's metaphors. On the day when everything will be good for the people of Israel, Isaiah says that 'the light of the moon will be as the light of the sun, and the light of the sun will be sevenfold, as the light of the seven days, in the day when the Lord binds up the hurt of his people and heals the wounds inflicted by his blow'.[38] The moon that shines like the sun could be easily imagined as Passover's night of the full moon. Similarly, the sevenfold light of the sun could be a poetical reworking of the sun in its ascending spring equinoctial aspect during the seven days of Passover. To a certain extent even his words 'in the day when the Lord binds up the hurt of his people and heals the wounds inflicted by his blow' are reminiscent of the exodus salvation theme.[39]

---

36. Yahweh commands it to stand still (Josh. 10.12–13) or not to rise at all (Job 9.6–7).

37. Philo, *Spec. Leg.* II, 151, 155.

38. Isa. 30.26.

39. From this perspective one is almost tempted to suggest that the pharaoh from the story of exodus is a personification of the sun whom Yahweh replaces as the decisive player in the drama of life and death on the night of Passover. One of the titles that pharaohs held was the son of Re, the sun god.

One might argue that the passage could equally refer to Tabernacles because some of its rites were also performed under the full moon, and furthermore because it was a very joyful occasion accompanied by singing which Isaiah also mentions.[40] However, the metaphor of the sevenfold light of the sun, in particular because it is combined with a moon that shines like the sun, could have been only drawn from Passover when the equinoctial sun was supposed to bring longer days and brighter light. The sun at Tabernacles, which took place during the month of the autumn equinox, was already in decline and the days were getting shorter and were losing their summer brilliance. Later tradition also confirms that Isaiah's metaphor derives from the time of Passover. 'The blessing of the sun',[41] the rarest synagogue service, formulated in the third century CE and performed only every 28 years, ends with these verses from Isaiah, but, more importantly, it takes place in Nisan, the month of the vernal equinox and Passover.

The previous discussion points out that in the search for the meaning of the season marked by Passover one has to explore the connotative scope of light as a symbol. In the Old Testament light has a variety of meanings. It symbolizes life,[42] salvation,[43] happiness,[44] Yahweh himself[45] or his word.[46] Its principal meaning, however, of which the aforementioned examples are only derivatives, is order. In Genesis, light is the first ordered form of the cosmos, the first structure that Yahweh creates[47] and on which depends the creation of every other element that is to be part of the ordered world. Even life presupposes light. It represents the act of creation, the act of establishing the world as an ordered complex.

From the perspective of natural cycles and seasonal changes, light and its natural manifestation, the sunlight, have additional symbolic functions. They are symbols of not just the cosmic order in general, but also of all the natural forces that are effective in maintaining that order. Among the variety of natural cycles, only the rhythm of light cycles, the moon's waxing and waning, the exchange between day and night and finally the equinoctial/solsticial changes has a permanent stability. Rains can be late or prolonged, summers can be cold or wet, winters dry and warm. As a

40. Isa. 30.29: You shall have a song as in the night when a holy feast is kept; and gladness of heart, as when one sets out to the sound of the flute to go to the mountain of the Lord, to the Rock of Israel.

41. Nulman 1993: 100. There is a printing omission of the number 20 in Nulman's entry so instead of every '28 years' it reads 'eight'.

42. Ps. 36.9.

43. Ps. 97.11.

44. Isa. 9.2.

45. Ps. 2.1; Isa. 60.19–20.

46. Ps. 119, 105; Isa. 2.3–5.

47. Gen. 1.2–3.

consequence of the regularity and the stability with which light cycles occur, light as a symbol is in opposition to every other cyclic natural phenomenon whose time of expected occurrence or disappearance is potentially volatile. Within the context of seasonal symbolism, light and sunlight are the ultimate symbols of nature as a constructive, beneficial order. Their natural antipodes, the night and darkness, therefore do not only symbolize primordial chaos because darkness is one of the elements of the world before creation, but also every other natural force whose cycle might become disordered or chaotic. Around the time of the vernal equinox when the relationship between day and night is more or less in balance, when the length of the day begins to equal that of the night to finally overtake it in duration, the light symbolism of the sun obviously becomes even more specific as the supremacy of day and light over night and darkness, or in other words, of the dominance of the forces of order over those which are in some aspect perceived as actually or latently detrimental to the continuity of the cosmos as a beneficial order.

Being observed at this particular time of the year, Passover as a rite of passage obviously had the role to close the period marked by domination of night and open the one in which the benevolent forces of the orderly world, symbolized by the rule of the daily light, prevailed. The time when the real world became an equivalent of the original creation, an actualized paradigm of the cosmic order, arrived with spring and the vernal equinox.

A similar understanding underlined the Babylonian Akitu festival. It was observed during the same month as Passover and one of the most important parts of its ceremonies was the reciting of *Enuma Elish*, the epic of creation which describes the struggle and victory of cosmic order over chaos. The latter Jewish traditions also give credence to the interpretation that the month of the vernal equinox and Passover had the meaning of introducing an ordered part of the year. Events such as blocking of the waters of the deep on the day of creation and appearance of the light of creation, which both represent subjugation and taming of the forces of primordial chaos, are thought to have happened on the date of Passover.[48]

According to the Bible, this springtime equinoctial opening of the period of order that was marked by Passover occurred during the 'first month'. Most often this expression is discussed in terms of its calendar value and whether it can be taken as an indicator that the beginning of a new calendar year was in spring. However, when the nature of events which the Bible connects with this specific month is considered it becomes obvious that as a time designation the expression 'first month' does not have great chronological merits and is mostly symbolic. The majority of those events represent, either in cosmic, theological or historical terms, a

48.   Smith 1987: 84.

new beginning. The flood ends in the first month.[49] The Israelites gain their freedom when they leave Egypt in the first month.[50] During the same month they arrive into the promized land.[51] The tabernacle, as a sign that Yahweh is now their god, is erected in the first month.[52] Hezekiah starts repairing the desecrated and abandoned temple in the first month.[53] As a sign of a new beginning, Ezra, the law giver, and the exiles leave Babylon in the first month.[54] After they arrive in Jerusalem, men married to foreign women separate from them by the first month.[55] And finally, in Ezekiel, Yahweh demands for his temple to be cleansed in the first month.[56] It is obvious that in these instances the 'first month' is not a calendric or chronological tool, but a symbolic one, immanently associated with the idea of a beginning.

However, there is a twist to this otherwise straightforward connection between the concepts of 'first month' and a beginning. The new times opened by the first month are represented as qualitatively different to the periods that precede them. In most cases the two are in stark contrast. Some of them are connected with Passover (leaving of Egypt, arrival into the promized land, Hezekiah's restoration of the temple), and we have already discussed their meaning in the context of the symbolic role that Passover plays in narratives. However, we find the same contrasting situations in other events that are said to have also taken place in the 'first month' and which are not explicitly connected with Passover. Given that in both cases the role of the 'first month' parallels that of Passover in narratives, it is obvious that this particular month also serves as an indicator of a period of transition. Furthermore, as in Passover, the new situation is always represented as positive change. The 'first month' symbolizes a time during which new, beneficial developments take place (exodus, the arrival into Canaan, the erecting of the tabernacle, departure from Babylon) and the time in which natural, social or religious retrogressions and departures from the desirable standards are corrected (the ending of flood, Hezekiah's restoration of the temple, the separation from foreign women, the cleansing of the temple). As in the case of the vernal equinox, the 'first month' also signals that a period of beneficial order is at hand.

The main question in this context is what made this particular season of the natural year to be comprehended as heralding a time of order, the idea

49. Gen. 8.13.
50. Num. 33.3.
51. Josh. 4.19.
52. Exod. 40.17.
53. 2 Chron. 29.3.
54. Ezra 7.9; 8.31.
55. Ezra 10.17.
56. Ezek. 45.18.

that, as we have seen, is central in the symbolic representations of Passover's position with respect to seasons. The answer to this question is given in the third designation for the time of Passover, the month of Abib, the month of the 'ears of corn' or, in other words, the beginning of the harvest. In Palestine, the harvest season commences during the vernal equinoctial month and it is an agrarian understanding of reality that is behind the order symbolism both of the sun and the first month. It is the period of food gathering and storing, of ensuring the survival of the community that is translated into an ultimate manifestation of order.

The story of the flood and its symbolic employment of particular months as indicators of the progressing and regressing chaos are perhaps the best evidence of how influential was the agrarian worldview as the source from which the biblical symbolic references of order were drawn. Much has been said about the dates of the beginning (seventeenth of the second month) and respectively the end (twenty-seventh of the second month of the next year) of the flood and their significance in representing the exact number of days in a solar year, but little attention, if any, has been paid to the actual sequence of months through which the flood events unfold and the meaning they add to the story.

According to Gen. 7.11 the devastating rains begin in the second month. Placing the beginning of the watery destruction in this particular month might appear an arbitrary choice, but we shall see that it actually has a very definite purpose which becomes clear when one adopts a farmer's perspective in reasoning about recurrent cycles of natural phenomena. As we know, Passover is celebrated in the first month, which is also the month Abib in which the ears of the barley are standing and the beginning of the harvest is immediate. The second month in which the 'fountains of the deep burst forth and windows of the heavens were opened'[57] is therefore the most critical period in the agricultural year when harvesting, threshing and storing of the grain are in full swing. It is the month that is the culmination of the long, arduous and most often anxiety-permeated process of growing corn. During this period, even rain, let alone flood, is a very harsh punishment for those whose existence depends on agriculture. In 1 Sam. 12.17–18, Samuel wants to teach the people to fear Yahweh and in order to demonstrate God's destructive powers he threatens that Yahweh will send rain and thunder which will ruin the harvest: 'Is it not wheat harvest today? I will call upon the Lord, that he may send thunder and rain; So Samuel called upon the Lord, and the Lord sent thunder and rain that day; and all the people greatly feared the Lord and Samuel'. A similar notion is behind the idea that flood begins in the second month. By designating this particular month as the time when the devastating rains begin, the narrator amplifies and further

---

57.   Gen. 7.11.

dramatizes the meaning of flood as a complete devastation and destruction. In doing this he obviously relies on a farmer's experience and wisdom regarding heavy rains in harvest season. A downpour that begins in the second month, that is after the vernal equinox, when the sun and dry conditions should prevail and the vegetation is in full bloom and after the harvest has commenced thereby ending the period of trepidation and anxiety regarding the growing crops, is a metaphor that from the farmer's perspective speaks of complete ruin and disorder. The same idea is obviously behind the emphasis placed on the seventh month as the time during which the waters begin to recede and the land re-emerges,[58] because in the agricultural calendar this is the month in which the first rains of the wet season are expected and the earth should not be drying up, but, quite conversely, it should begin to be saturated in preparation for ploughing.

The symbolic picture of reversing to the conditions of the primeval chaos is built not only on the ideas of the flood and the annihilation of all life, but also through the complete reversal of the order of natural seasons. Only when this backward motion of the yearly cycle of seasons is brought to the point of its beginning is the cosmic order re-established. That point, however, is given as twofold, as the first month, and as the second month. Gen. 8.13–14: (13) 'In the six hundred and first year, in the first month, the first day of the month, the waters were dried from off the earth; and Noah removed the covering of the ark, and looked, and behold, the face of the ground was dry. (14) In the second month, on the twenty-seventh day of the month, the earth was dry.' At first glance the duality of dates seems perplexing and possibly a result of different traditions and the failure of the final redactors to harmonize the text. However, such an explanation can hardly be justified. First, because the two verses in which the different months (and dates) are mentioned are too close to each other and so clearly in conflict that an accidental omission to erase one of them is almost out of the question. Second, because both the verse 13 and the verse 14 correspond with Gen. 7.11 which determines the time of the beginning of the rains. 'In the six hundredth year of Noah's life, in the second month, on the seventeenth day of the month, on that day all the fountains of the great deep burst forth, and the windows of the heavens were opened.' The version with the first month relates to Noah's years; the second month version with the precise dating. And finally, because redactorial changes and scribes' errors do not clarify the reasons why exactly the second month was the preferred choice for the beginning of the deluge. If the only concern of the author was to report that the flood lasted 365 days, the exact number of days in a solar year, he could have

---

58. Gen. 8.4.

had the beginning in any month whatsoever and the effect would have been the same.

Instead of splintering the text into different traditions, revisions, editions and so on, it is more rational to assume that, despite their seemingly inconsistent character, both versions are there with a purpose and that both carry some message about the main theme of the story of the flood, that of chaos and order. The storyteller obviously wanted to have a full cycle of disorder of twelve months, so naturally having placed its beginning in the month in which the watery chaos would have the most destructive effect, the month of harvest, that is the second month, he had to also end the deluge in the same month of the next year. However, this obviously contradicted the idea that cosmos and order are re-established in the first month with the arrival of dry weather and the beginning of harvest, so, in a true Solomonic tradition the solution was found in having the flood ending simultaneously in both months. Most probably, neither the author nor the readers saw anything disputable about it because the numerical designations of months in the Bible had symbolic and not calendric value.

The flood story is a complex story conveying many messages. The one about the re-establishment of order stems from an agricultural understanding and conceptions of what constitutes order or disorder. Having the period of harvest as paradigmatic of order does not mean on the other hand that the rainy period of the year, which in the agricultural scheme of works corresponds to the ploughing season, was perceived as bad or disordered. It was also part of the higher cosmological order of things in which 'seedtime and harvest, cold and heat, summer and winter, day and night' alternate.[59] The harmonious nature of the alternating two halves of the natural year was also ritually expressed by placing on each sabbath twelve loaves of bread in two layers of six on the golden table in the temple.[60] The Bible, as in many other cases, does not explain the reasons for this particular ritual, but Philo connects it with the equinoctial dichotomy of the year.[61]

At the very concrete level of day-to-day living, however, the two seasons were very differently experienced. The winter brought the discomfort of cold weather, long nights and constant worries regarding the coming of the rains, their sufficiency for the proper development of seeds and the growth of the stalks. Above all, it was marked by gradual

---

59.   Gen. 8.22.

60.   Lev. 24.5–8.

61.   'But on each seventh day loaves are exposed on the holy table equal in number to the months of the year in two layers of six each, each layer corresponding to the equinoxes. For there are two equinoxes in each year, in spring and autumn, with intervals, the sum of which is six months.' Philo. *Spec. Leg.* I, 172.

depletion of food reserves and uneasiness as to whether they would last until the next yield of grains was ripe enough to be harvested. The anxieties reached a climax near winter's end, immediately before harvest because it was the time when the question of survival was to be decided. According to the Mishnah, a judgment on grain is delivered on Passover, that is during the month when barley, the first ripe grain, is ready or almost ready to be reaped.[62] The time immediately before Passover was the hungriest part of the year[63] when supplies from the previous harvest were at their lowest level while the new crops were not yet ripe enough.[64] If anything went wrong in the order of seasonal changes at this stage, even if everything had gone well with the rains, the threat of hunger and starvation[65] was immediate.[66] From this perspective the end of the rain season was an extremely hazardous time[67] and we shall see later that this sensation of danger found its actual ritual expression during Passover.

The dry season, during which the period of the grain harvest was the most important, also had its uncertainties, but nevertheless everyday living was easier and safer. There was plenty of food and everyone was warm. [68] As in the words of Solomon: 'for lo, the winter is past, the rain is over and gone. The flowers appear on the earth, the time of singing has come.'[69] The harvest brought relief from the anxieties of the winter season. For Jeremiah, harvest is the time of salvation: 'The harvest is past, the summer is ended, and we are not saved.'[70] The connection between the season of harvest and the notion of delivery from danger was in the Exodus story translated into ideological concepts. The pharaoh and Egypt in general took on the threatening aspects of the period preceding the

62. The Mishnah, *Rosh Hashanah* 1.2.B. Neusner 1988: 299.

63. In many cultures the names of the months that precede the harvest imply hunger. In Greece the coloquial names for April allude to shaking the empty bread box and choking of hunger. Brumfield 1981: 36. In Sawzi culture, December is the month before the first crops ripen and is called 'to swallow the pickings of the teeth'. Smith 1982: 121.

64. In this context it is not superfluous to note that after the ritual cutting of the first sheaf during Passover the Jerusalem market was full of parched grain, which was probably a welcome temporary addition to a diet relying on depleted food reserves.

65. Philo qualifies starvation as 'the most intolerable of sufferings'. Philo, *Spec. Leg.* II, 201.

66. According to the economist Sen, famine, defined as a sudden decline in availability of food, in subsistence economies always comes as a result either of drought, flood or some other cataclysm. Sen 1976 in Caplan 1992: 19.

67. Citing rabbinic literature, E. Zareen-Zohar gives a summery of the complex set of climatic phenomena on which depended the success of the harvest. Among the dangers were blasting winds, noxious dews, scorching heat and rains. Zareen-Zohar 1999: 72–73.

68. In the Proverbs summer and harvest are the times when food and sustenance are gathered. Prov. 6.7–8.

69. Song 2.11–12.

70. Jer. 8.20.

harvest, Yahweh replaced the harvest, while rescue from starvation became liberation from slavery. Even the oncoming abundance of the harvest found its translation as the gold the Israelites get from the Egyptians.[71]

The difference in the existential realities translated into an asymmetric perception of these two seasons with respect to the idea of order. For the functioning of the cosmos both seasons were indeed necessary, but from the perspective of human existence, winter appeared as less orderly in comparison to summer.[72] With its abundant food supply and warm weather, summer was the desired standard and that is the reason why we find symbols of order in close association with the beginning of this season. From this particular angle, order appears as nothing else but an idealized projection of the natural conditions of the dry period. As a ritual of passage, Passover no doubt played a crucial role in ensuring that the order in which everyone is satiated and warm takes hold. After the temple was destroyed, the function of Passover to introduce the time of order was even literally expressed as 'seder' – order.

The asymmetric perception of the seasons found its expression through cultic practice as well. The preservation of only three seasonal observances in the Bible indicates that before Passover was given a different meaning and was thereby separated from the other two, the three festivals formed a cultic cycle, a firmly connected and coherent system[73] built around a common leitmotif.[74] With respect to seasons, both Passover and Tabernacles served as their passage points and from this perspective there was no difference between their functions as opening and closing festivals. However, when they are viewed as parts of a system it becomes clear that the cycle started with Passover, continued through Weeks and ended with Tabernacles and that the common thread that connected them was their reference to the summer season and the special understanding of

---

71. Exod. 11.1–2; 12.35–36.

72. In Philo's words: 'But the month of the autumnal equinox, though first in order as measured by the course of the sun, is not called first in the law, because at that time all the fruits have been gathered in and the trees are shedding their leaves and all the bloom which the spring brought in its prime already scorched by the heat of the summer sun is wilting under the dry currents of air. And so to give the name of "first" to a month in which both uplands and lowlands are sterilized and unfruitful seemed to him altogether unsuitable and incongruous. For things which come first and head the list should be associated with all the fairest and most desirable things which are the sources of birth and increase to animals and fruits and plants, not with the processes of destruction and the dark thoughts which it suggests.' *Spec. Leg.* II, 153–54.

73. Smith argues that the meaning of individual rites can be comprehended only if they are viewed as part of a particular ritual system. Smith 1982: 103–112.

74. As K. Stevenson's discussion on festivities of Holy Week testifies, moments of sacred time that are spread across seasons are often seen as different chapters in the same story. Stevenson 1988: 9.

it that we already considered above. Within the tripartite festival system and its connection with the summer period of the year, Passover represented a double opening. It opened the natural season that would be closed six months later with Tabernacles and also one of its sub-periods, the agricultural season of the corn harvest, the closure of which happened during the Festival of Weeks, when the first fruits of the cereal harvest were presented at the temple after ceremonial counting of 49 days or seven weeks of reaping from the second day of Passover and the cutting of the very first sheaf of barley of the new harvest season. Tabernacles concluded the cycle of summer. Although the autumn festival included rites of drawing and pouring water over the altar which undoubtedly point to its connection with the rainy season, in the Bible it is called 'feast of ingathering',[75] the feast when all the produce of the land is stored, and olives and grapes pressed, which clearly indicates that within the festival system its function was to close and finalize the summer period of food gathering. Philo also understood the function of Tabernacles with respect to seasons as a closure rather than an opening. Moreover, he also refers to the period of food gathering as the main object of that function.[76] Another important indication that the three festivals formed a strictly defined sequence in which Passover was the opening act while Tabernacles its conclusion is the difference in the requirements for the participation of the common people in the temple ceremonies. During Tabernacles that involvement was required for a full seven days; at Passover, however, the active involvement of the public in the temple rites was expected and limited only to the first day. The next temple gathering took place on Weeks.

The character which the Israelites attributed to the periods that Passover opened can be also investigated through the symbolism of the number seven which plays a prominent role in the organization of each of the three festivals and serves as a crucial link that connects the festival system. Both Passover and Tabernacles lasted for seven days beginning on the night that rounded off a cycle of the waxing moon, which in the lunar month is roughly 14 days, two weeks or symbolically two sevens. Weeks festival was connected to Passover by the seven weeks (7x7) that were accounted for from its second day, while Tabernacles took place in the seventh month from Passover.

In the Old Testament the number seven is never literally used as a mere quantifying unit without some special meaning attached to it. Seven days is the period which most of the rites of separation, initiation and purification require. Menstruating women and those with bodily

---

75. Exod. 23.16; 34.22; Deut. 16.13.
76. Philo, *Spec. Leg.* II, 213.

discharge are unclean for seven days.[77] All kind of diseases necessitate a seven-day separation.[78] Those in contact with dead bodies are also unclean for seven days.[79] The ordination of priests lasts seven days,[80] first-born of animals are sacrificed on the eighth day after birth,[81] with the circumcision of boys following the same pattern.[82] Solomon builds the temple in seven years.[83] In these cases the number seven conveys the meaning of completeness, fullness of the cycle. In this sense the seven days of Passover and the seven days of Tabernacles symbolized that their own ritual time was a complete cycle and that the natural seasons for which they served as dividers were properly separated by a complete, perfect transition period. The Feast of Weeks, for example, was celebrated for only one day because it closed a sub-period in the natural season and as such it did not require the full seven-day period. It was just an extension of Passover. The number seven also had transformative powers; it ushered in positive changes. In order to capture Jericho, seven priests with seven trumpets were ordered to walk seven times round the city walls on the seventh day. A child sneezed seven times and was restored to life.[84] Naaman the leper bathed seven times in the Jordan and was cleansed.[85] The seven days of Passover and Tabernacles therefore also symbolized a fresh and positive start with respect to the seasons they opened.

The two festivals were also part of a bigger cycle of seven, that of the cycle of months. Passover happened in the first month, or at the beginning of the cycle, while Tabernacles took place in the seventh month and in this sense it represented a closure of the cultic cycle. The seventh day, the seventh month or the seventh year, apart from representing the wholeness of the cycle, also represent a closure, a finalization, an ending to a period. God made the world in six days, but on the seventh he rested.[86] Slaves serve for six years, but in the seventh they are released.[87] Debts are remembered for six years, but in the seventh they are forgiven.[88] The land is worked for six years, but in the seventh it is left to rest.[89] From this perspective the year consisted not of two symmetrical seasons of six

77. Lev. 15.13, 19.
78. Lev. 14.1–37.
79. Num. 19.11, 16.
80. Exod. 29.35.
81. Exod. 22.30.
82. Gen. 17.12.
83. 1 Kgs 6.38.
84. 2 Kgs 4.35.
85. 2 Kgs 5.14.
86. Gen. 2.2.
87. Deut. 15.12.
88. Deut. 15.1.
89. Lev. 25.4.

months each, but of one period of seven months, between the first and the seventh month, from Passover to Tabernacles, symbolic of completeness and perfection, and another of five months between Tabernacles and Passover that was less perfect.

Within the seven-month cycle of perfection, the period that was symbolically represented as the most consummate and the most complete, because it was always desired to be such, was the period of the corn harvest, the closure of which happened after seven cycles of seven days (7x7) were finished and which was celebrated on the fiftieth day as the Feast of Weeks. The same structure of 7x7 was replicated in establishing the year of jubilee,[90] which was, as the name says, the year of celebrations and rejoicing. The latter provides powerful evidence of the enormous importance of the period of harvest and the joy with which its successful end was celebrated.

The individual elements involved in the symbolism of its general time indicates that Passover as a rite of passage opened a period which was comprehended as the season of order, salvation and perfection. The understanding is a symbolic translation of the significance that the agricultural perception of the world and nature assigns to the season of harvest and generally the season of food gathering and storing.

3.2.2. *Time of the Rituals*

In contrast to the general aspect of Passover where we had the sun and the daily light as dominant symbols, in the time organization of its individual rites we encounter their opposites, the night and the moon as the purveyors of the symbolic meanings. Each of the two rituals that we know about, the eating of the sacrificial animal and the cutting of the first sheaf of barley, had nocturnal associations.

However, despite having the night as the shared theme of their ritual times, the meaning of night in the context of eating of the sacrificial animal was not the same as the one in the context of cutting of the first sheaf.

The eating of the sacrificial animal had an exclusively nocturnal character and all of its individual acts, the killing, the roasting, the eating and finally the disposal of the remains, had to be completed in the course of a single night. Given its unique date, the ritual clearly had also very strong lunar associations. The 14th[91] was the date of the full moon, an obviously important and meaningful occasion even in ordinary, non-festival times.

In contrast to the intensely nocturnal orientation of the ritual time of

---

90.   Lev. 25.8.

91.   Exod. 12.6; Lev. 23.5; Num. 9.3; Deut. 16.6; Ezra 45.21. The Israelites counted the beginning of the month from the first sighting of the new moon.

the eating of the sacrificial animal, the time structure of the first sheaf involved both parts of the day. The initial act, the opening of the ritual itself, happened during day time, while the night was reserved for its central and closing acts, the ceremonial reaping of the previously prepared sheaves and their presentation in the temple. According to the Mishnah, the ritual began on the afternoon of the 14th and finished during the second night of the festival.[92] The Bible does not give any direct information regarding the time structure of cutting of the first sheaf, but an indirect reference to it is perhaps contained in the story of Joseph's dreams. The first dream involves binding of sheaves, an activity that was also performed as part of the ritual, as a matter of fact as its opening act, whereas the dream that followed featured the sun, the moon and the stars,[93] the respective luminaries and rulers of the two parts of the day during which the actual ritual activities took place.

The time structure and apportioning of the individual acts of the cutting of the first sheaf that is, unlike the ritual of eating the sacrificial animal and its nocturnal exclusiveness, divided between the two parts of the day indicates that the key to unlock the specific meaning of night within the setting of this particular ritual setting cannot be found only within the symbolic scope of night as such, but rather as part of the night/day relation, that is the relation between the parts of the day that make up the ritual time framework. And if we accept that there is a possibility, even a remote one, that Joseph's dreams have some connection with this ritual, then that relation appears to be of a complementary nature rather than antithetical, given that the second dream refers to the light-bringing forces, an aspect shared by the night and the day. In other words, revealing the specific meaning of the night in the case of the cutting of the first sheaf will depend on finding the meaning that both the night and the day possibly had in common with respect to harvest, the main concern of the ritual itself.

In the case of the ritual of eating the sacrificial animal, the exclusiveness of the night of the full moon as the only possible time for the performance of all of its individual acts indicates that the specific meaning of night in this context rests entirely within the symbolic scope of night as such and without any references or relation to day time except as its antithesis. Consequently, the meaning of the full moon also has to be interpreted from within that particular and exclusive symbolism of night, as an answer to the question, what is the nature and the meaning of the night/moonlight relation from the perspective of the symbolic references that are unique to night?

In the Bible, night is one of those dynamic symbols that incorporates

---

92. The Mishnah, *Menahot* 10.3. Neusner 1988: 753–54.
93. Gen. 37.5–9.

numerous meanings and provides a wealth of contradictions. Its symbolic references are further complicated by its relationship with the moon, which is governed by the particularities of the reality of the moon itself and which makes the nature of that relationship much more complex and diversified than the one between the sun and the day which we had as part of the seasonal symbolism of Passover.

As part of the daily pattern,[94] night belongs to the cosmos, the created world of regular cycles. Like the sunlit part of the day, it also has its luminary and, regardless of how weak its light might be in comparison to that of the sun, it is nevertheless a sign of the act of creation. Together with the stars, the moon rules over night and is a manifestation of the forces of order.[95] Its light is described as splendour[96] and glory[97] and compared with a girl's beauty[98] and righteousness.[99] Nevertheless, the moon is a subject of recurrent waxing and waning and downright disappearance from the sky which makes the nightly light much less constant and reliable in comparison to its daily counterpart. This fact also reflects negatively on the character of the night itself. It permanently associates it with darkness, one of the elements from the period before the establishment of the cosmos which in the Bible most often serves as a metaphor for an utmost horror and an antithesis of anything good. It is a symbol of evil,[100] misfortune,[101] punishment,[102] damnation and death.[103] When it is disassociated from the moon and its light, night is an agency through which this menacing element of primordial chaos finds its expression in the world of order.[104] In the words of the Psalmist: 'Thou makest darkness and it is night, when all the beast of the forest creep forth.'[105] As such, night is in the Bible the prime time of murderers, thieves, adulterers,[106] a time of anxieties,[107] fears and uncertainties.[108] Within the setting of this entirely negative aspect of the night, the moonlight has the role of the guardian against all the chaotic or possibly chaotic forces, epitomized by darkness, and the destructive effects that

94.   Gen. 1.2–3.
95.   Ps. 136.9.
96.   Job 31.26.
97.   Isa. 24.23; Isa. 60.19.
98.   Song 6.10.
99.   Job 25.4–5.
100. Job 30.26.
101. Job 19.8.
102. Job 18.18.
103. Job 10.22; Amos 5.18–20.
104. Gen. 2.5.
105. Ps. 104.20.
106. Job 24.14–15.
107. Job 7.4b.
108. Job 27.20.

their encroachment beyond allowed limits might have on the world of order, irrespective of whether that order manifests as social, religious or natural. Among nights, which are *per se* a window of opportunity for the intrusion of chaotic elements into the ordered world, the worst are the dark and moonless nights, while the nights of the full moon are the time when their negative influences are most curtailed.

This function of being the gateway through which the destructive powers gain access and make themselves present in the world of order is a symbolic dimension that is unique to night and as such the aspect that we earlier said is needed to understand the specific meaning of night in the context of the ritual of eating the sacrificial animal. The time of this ritual, because of its undivided nocturnal orientation, primarily symbolizes and refers to the elements of the primordial chaos. The first night of Passover, despite the light of the full moon, is therefore symbolically the darkest and the most threatening among all other nights because it exemplifies the externalization of the elements of primordial chaos. In this symbolic setting the full moon and the light it sheds serve only as a counterbalance against the chaotic forces that night as such embodies, as a security against their unpredictable and volatile nature that vouchsafes the perpetuation of the established cosmic order.

There is one characteristic of the ritual of eating of the sacrificial animal that strongly supports our claim that the first night of Passover reflects the ultimately negative dimensions of night symbolism. The ritual had a form of an all-night vigil,[109] a special course of action that is in the Bible undertaken predominantly as a response to situations that are perceived as critical or dangerous. David spends whole nights in supplication for the life of his child.[110] Samuel also stays awake praying for advice from Yahweh as what to do with Saul who disobeyed the Lord's commandment.[111] And Jeremiah calls out on the Israelites to arise and pray during the night for the lives of their children who are starving.[112]

Vigils, even when not ritually performed like the aforementioned examples, obviously symbolize precarious times. Their atmosphere is charged with uncertainty, tension and anxious anticipation. The same dramatic aura surrounds the night of the tenth plague, the event that is represented as the motive for establishing Passover as a festival. It is a most violent time, a night of indiscriminate killing of all firstborn, during which only a mark on the doorposts separates the Israelites from

---

109.   Exod. 12.42. It was a night of watching by the LORD, to bring them out of the land of Egypt; so this same night is a night of watching kept to the LORD by all the people of Israel throughout their generations.

110.   2 Sam. 12.15–16.

111.   1 Sam. 15.10–12.

112.   Lam. 2.19.

death. However, when the symbolic tension, drama and anxious anticipation are placed within the firmly defined seasonal context of Passover, it is clear that the message about danger that is contained in the symbolism of this night refers to the actual time of the year in which the ritual of eating the sacrificial animal took place. That particular time, as we have said before, corresponded with the opening stages of the harvest season, or, in terms of existential realities, the hungriest and therefore also the most dangerous part of the year. The ritual was doubtlessly performed in order to protect the crops thereby ensuring the survival of the people. Its observance time, the night of the full moon, communicated the message of crisis, of danger that might come from forces that are detrimental for the outcome of the harvest, but also of hope that the 'fruits of the ground' will be good and plentiful, that the established cosmic order is still in place and that the chaos will not be allowed to overstep its bounds. The danger is symbolized by the night, the hope by the full moon.

However, as we said earlier, the symbolic scope of night time does not include only connotations with sinister overtones. In the Bible, night is also the principal time of encounters and happenings that are from the perspective of the human ability to comprehend them shrouded in mystery and secrecy rather than outright and clear danger. The strange episode of Jacob's wrestling contest with Yahweh in Gen. 32.24–31 happens at night. Manna, the miracle food, falls at night.[113] Yahweh prefers the night as the appropriate time to communicate his messages[114] and, moreover, even chooses to dwell in darkness,[115] the inseparable symbolic companion of night, or to appear surrounded by thick darkness.[116] As the time when events that are beyond the limits of human understanding, night is intimately connected with fertility and related concepts given that life creation was for the biblical authors a secret that only Yahweh could know. He is the one who opens wombs[117] and he is the one who breathes life into a child inside a womb.[118]

In Job the union between night and fertility is openly and unambiguously identified. Overwhelmed by his misfortunes, Job curses: 'Let the day perish wherein I was born, and the night which said, "A man-child is

---

113. Num. 11.9.
114. Gen. 20.3; 26.24; 28.10–16; 31.24; 46.2; Exod. 12.31; Num. 22.2; Judg. 7.9; 1 Kgs 3.5.
115. 1 Kgs 8.12; 2 Chron. 6.11.
116. Deut. 4.11; 5.22–23.
117. Gen. 29.31; 30.22.
118. Eccl. 11.5: As you do not know how the spirit comes to the bones in the womb of a woman with child, so you do not know the work of God who makes everything. Ps. 139.13: For thou didst form my inward parts, thou didst knit me together in my mother's womb.

conceived."[119] 'Yea, let that night be barren.'[120] Of the two parts of the day, night is the one which has the priority of being the fertile time and is the one that presides over the judgment whether life will be conceived. Like the first cosmic structure, the light, which is created out of the unfathomable darkness, the beginnings of life are enveloped and shrouded in the mysteries of the night.

However, that positive, life-giving aspect of the night as the fecund womb is not in itself enough for life to be realized, to become existence. It remains only a mere potentiality if the part that the night plays in the process of life creation is not complemented by that of the sunlit portion of the day. The night is the time when life is created, the time of germination and gestation, but only with the arrival of the morning and the daylight will that potentiality of life be born into actual life, become life itself.[121] In the words of the Psalmist, 'From the womb of the morning, like dew your youth shall come forth.'[122] Only when they function as one, as a complementary pair that reciprocates each other's role in the creation of life, do the night and the day function as effective fertilizing and fruit-bearing powers. In Deuteronomy the fruitfulness of the plants is directly linked to both of them. The sun and the moon are represented as performing the same task. 'Blessed by the Lord be his land, ... with the choicest fruits of the sun, and the rich yield of the moons...'[123] In his critique of the cult of the sun and the moon, Philo also refers to their complementary nature in maintaining the fecundity of animals, plants and fruits.[124] He also interprets the daily offering of two lambs, one sacrificed at dawn, the other at dusk,[125] as thank offerings for respectively the benefactions of the day time and the night time.[126]

Almost as if it were a counterpoint to the dread of the first night of Passover and its ritual, it is this life-giving, auspicious dimension of the night that we encounter in the day/night-time structure of the cutting of the first sheaf of barley. In this case, night does not have sinister references as a hiatus through which the primordial chaos creeps upon the cosmos. It

119.   Job 3.3.
120.   Job 3.7.
121.   Job 3.16; Ps. 58.8b.
122.   Ps. 110.3b.
123.   Deut. 33.14. The revised edition translates moons as months, but in Hebrew the two concepts are related given that month is a lunation and are both expressed with one word, *yerah*.
124.   Philo, *Spec. Leg.* I, 16. 'For those who see the sun with its advances and retreats producing the yearly seasons in which the animals and plants and fruits are brought at fixed periods of time from their birth to maturity, and the moon as handmaid and successor to the sun taking over at night the care and supervision of all that he had charge of by day...'
125.   Num. 28.3–5.
126.   Philo, *Spec. Leg.* I, 169.

symbolizes the pulsating cycles through which the cosmos demonstrates its ordering nature and through which it functions as a created, meaningful world. And that life-endorsing nocturnal symbolism is in perfect harmony with the purpose of the ritual, the release of the harvest for common use.

Given that purpose, it is very tempting to interpret the night of this ritual as the conclusion to the dark, gestational period of the crops before they were born into the light of the day and the harvesting season or, in other words, before they became life for the people. The ritual cutting would then represent severing of the crops from the womb of the mother earth and that of the night-dominated season, the winter. The sequence of the performed acts, binding/cutting/presentation,[127] perhaps to some extent points in that direction because it does not follow the usual order of harvesting activities which calls first for the cutting of the stalks and only then for binding them into sheaves. The act of binding could be taken as preparation for the subsequent birth of the stalks through their separation/cutting from the earth.

However, finding an answer to the question of what this night and the ritual acts that were performed represented is not an overly important issue since they are probably just one of the numerous variations of the life and fertility motif. What is important, though, and what the sequence of the activities of this ritual reveals is that, although the preparation for the release of the harvest occurred on the afternoon preceding the first night of the festival, the actual cutting of the sheaves that symbolically released the harvest for public use had to wait until the second night, that is until the eating of the sacrificial animal was over. This unusual interlude between the ritual acts points out that the eating of the sacrificial animal was a prerequisite for the final acts of the cutting of the first sheaf. The anticipated blessings associated with the night of this ritual could become reality only after the danger symbolized by the night of eating the sacrificial animal was over. When this is taken into account the two rituals actually become one in which the sequence of activities is as follows: the preparation of sheaves for release; the ritual eating of the sacrificial animal; the cutting of the sheaves and the release of the harvest. What we are missing in this superimposed ritual in order to completely understand the orchestration and the interplay of its meanings is the objective of the second component, that is the eating of the sacrificial animal, with respect

---

127. The Mishnah, *Menahot* 10.3–4: 'How did they do it? Agents of the court go forth on the eve of [the afternoon before] the festival [of Passover]. And they make it into sheaves while it is still attached to the ground, so that it will be easy to reap. And all the villagers nearby gather together there [on the night after the first day of Passover] so that it will be reaped with great pomp. Once it gets dark [on the night of the 16th of Nisan] he says ... They reaped it, and they put it into baskets. They brought it to the court [of the Temple] ...' Neusner 1988: 753–54.

to the ultimate goal of the ritual, the release of the harvest. Our next main task and greatest challenge will be to see whether that objective can be inferred from its symbolic references.

3.3. *Symbolism of the First-Night Ritual*

In order to understand the objective of the ritual during the first night of Passover and the symbolic references of its individual elements such as the vigil, the act of eating, the attributes of the sacrifice and the treatment of the bones, we need an operational framework that will narrow the scope of possible interpretations. Most often such a framework is provided by the function of the ritual. However, given that unlike the cutting of the first sheaf, which was never a subject of Yahwistic ideological interest, the eating of the sacrificial animal was the sequence of the festival chosen to exemplify the new Yahwistic values, we do not have direct knowledge of that function. In order to retrieve it we shall have to rely on the arrangement and the characteristics of its components, the time, the space, the participants and, in our case, the sacrifice which is the focus of the whole ritual. So before we attempt to interpret the meaning of the individual elements and acts of the first-night ritual it is necessary to briefly discuss its structural characteristics.

3.3.1. *The Structure*

Despite its inconsistent presentation in the Bible the ritual actually keeps and presents a very stringently defined structure in terms of when, where and who performs the ritual. The clear outline of that structure, however, appears only when the rite is presented in its skeletal form, stripped of the literary and ideological embellishments which by emphasizing different aspects make it appear as if it had undergone some considerable historical changes that in texts reflect as different versions.

In terms of time,[128] the ritual commences with the setting of the sun[129] and ends with the arrival of the morning.[130] The night, as we already know, is the dangerous night of the full moon during the spring equinoctial month, the month of the beginning of the harvest. The initial act of killing the sacrificial animal is done in the evening. Everything else that follows, the preparation and eating of the flesh and the removal of the remains, has to be completed by morning.[131]

In terms of spatial organization, the ritual is always performed within a

---

128. For discussions on characteristics and quality of 'ritual time', see van der Leeuw 1938: 384–87; Eliade 1954: 51–92; 1959: 68–113; Grainger 1974: 107–43.
129. Exod. 12.6; Lev. 23.5; Num. 9.3, 5; Deut. 16.6; Josh. 5.10.
130. Exod. 34.25; Num. 9.12; Deut. 16.7; Josh. 5.11.
131. Exod. 12.10, 22; 23.18; 34.25; Num. 9.12; Deut. 16.4, 7.

very clearly defined space, whether it is the precincts of the temple[132] or within houses.[133] The perimeters of these enclosures obviously serve as demarcation lines that confine and separate the non-ritual from the ritual space. Delineation of a particular space is indicated even in the case of observances that are said to have happened even before building the permanent sanctuary which subsequently took over the role as the special cultic space. Before Joshua keeps the Passover in Gilgal, the marking of the special zone is indicated by setting up the twelve stones.[134] The Sinai Passover is celebrated in the tabernacle, the building of which precedes the celebration.[135] The ritual space either inherently implies cultic space, like the temple or the tabernacle, or has to be transformed into one by purification and consecration with blood as in the case of the Exodus Passover.[136]

In terms of participants, a person can take part in the rite on the first day only within a group setting and only as part of a group. The group is defined in a variety of ways such as fathers' houses, household or joined households,[137] people of Israel[138] or just quite indistinctly as many people,[139] holy convocation[140] or great assembly.[141] The specific setting in which the ritual eating takes place, on the other hand, should not be understood to mean that the rite was a communal feast in a sense that every member of the community actually participated in it. What its group character reveals is that its effectiveness depended on finishing the eating of the sacrificial animal during the span of a single night, a task that can be successfully completed only by a party of people.

The requirement for special clothes in which the emphasis is on the uniformity of dress[142] seems to indicate that not everyone could be a member of the group, given that wearing the same clothes or certain items, in our case staff and sandals, are usually a sign of membership in a group that is entrusted with specific duties or particular abilities.[143] The special membership is also indicated by the requirement for a special marking on

132. Deut. 16.5–6; 2 Chron. 30.1; 35.5–6; Ezek. 46.9.
133. Exod. 12.46.
134. Josh. 4.20–5.10.
135. Num. 8.22–9.2.
136. Exod. 12.7.
137. Exod. 12.3–4.
138. Num. 9.2; Josh. 5.10; 2. Chron. 35.17; Ezra 6.21.
139. 2 Chron. 30.13.
140. Lev. 23.7; Num. 28.18.
141. 2 Chron. 30.13.
142. Exod. 12.11.
143. According to Joseph, one of the functions of uniformity of dress is to minimize the possibility of confusing members with non-members. It solves problems with group boundaries. Joseph 1986: 66.

the hand and the forehead.[144] One of the special characteristics of the members refers to their gender. It seems that originally they were all men,[145] since even in the nationalistic context of the biblical texts which refer to 'people of Israel'[146] or 'congregation of Israel',[147] the only *sine qua non* of the people taking part in the ritual is circumcision, a clear reference to the male part of the population. The ordinance that even foreigners could take part in it provided they were circumcised[148] only further endorses its original neutrality with respect to ethnicity. Instead, it reveals that the ritual was related to the fertility cult, since the covenant regarding circumcision involves a fertility issue, namely a promise by Yahweh that Abraham will father numberless descendants.[149] The insistence on circumcision further reveals that the men participating in the ritual had to be sexually mature. According to Eilberg-Schwartz, who in many details explains the intimate connection between circumcision and fertility, circumcision entails sexual maturity[150] since it involves the proper functioning of sexual organs.[151] From this perspective, the members of the group performing the pre-commemorative rite do not appear to be members of the community in general, as it is usually regarded, but as very clearly defined in terms of age and gender, as adult men.[152]

When the characteristics of all of these three structural aspects – the time, the space, the participants – are combined it becomes clear that the ritual originally had very clear demarcation lines in every aspect and that the idea governing its performance was that a single group of men, gathered in one place, performed the rite during a single night. The centralizing tendencies of the cult in combination with the rising national significance attributed to the festival obfuscated many of the original boundaries that defined the ritual. The group character was preserved, but the gender and the age of the participants were redefined in line with the nationalistic agenda. The demand that the ritual be performed in the central sanctuary placed strain on its space boundaries, given that the temple courtyards could not accommodate everyone who could, accord-

---

144. Exod. 35.9.
145. Exod. 23.17; 34.23; Deut. 16.16.
146. Exod. 12.27; Num. 9.2, 4, 5; Josh. 5.10; 2 Kgs 23.22; 2 Chron. 35.17.
147. Exod. 12.3, 6, 47.
148. Exod. 12.48.
149. Gen. 17.1–11.
150. Philo also connects circumcision with fertility. Philo, *Spec. Leg.* I, 7.
151. By analogy immature trees are regarded as uncircumcised. Eilberg-Schwartz 1990: 141–54.
152. In the Temple Scroll a passage that refers to Passover forbids women and minors from taking part in this ritual and requires that the participants be at least 20 years old. The same prohibition can be found in *Jub.* 49.17.

ing to the new customs, be allowed to perform the ritual. The strain resulted in restricting only its beginning, the killing of the animal, to the temple's precincts, while the rest of the ritual acts, according to the Mishnah, had to be performed in other types of confined spaces.[153] At some stage even the time confines were relaxed allowing the burning of the remains to be done on the 16th of Nisan, that is on its third day.[154]

The centre of the ritual was its unique sacrifice. The ways of preparing its flesh for eating might have differed in different times, but throughout the biblical books Passover sacrifice is presented as singular and separate from any other sacrificial category. In some aspects it resembles the peace offering,[155] which also had to be eaten during the same day[156] and whose remains also had to be relatively swiftly disposed of.[157] However, the peace offering was not required to be eaten in a group setting, nor was the consumption required to be done at night, and in contrast to the flesh of the Passover animal that was completely consumed by the persons on whose behalf it was killed, part of the animal that was slaughtered as a peace offering always belonged to the priests.[158] Indeed, according to the historical books, for Passover even the priests had to provide an animal for themselves.[159] Also, neither peace offering nor any other type of sacrifice required a special treatment of the bones of the sacrificial animal as was the case with the bones of the Passover animals. It seems that in later times the Passover sacrifice tended to be confused with the peace offering, and the rabbis in the Mishnah went through a lot of strain to clarify the differences between them.[160] Their insistence that the only animals that can be accounted as valid Passover sacrifices are the ones killed under proper designation only further endorses its singularity.[161] Philo also fails to mention it as part of the sacrificial system.[162]

Its uniqueness left its trace in the language that the Bible uses in reference to the sacrificial animals. Although designating numerous and even different kinds of animals, the used expression is never given in the plural form. People 'kill the passover lamb'[163] and 'roast the passover lamb'.[164] This idiomatic use of the singular form is perhaps an indication

153. The Mishnah, *Pesaḥim* 5.5, A, B, C, D. Neusner 1988: 238.
154. The Mishnah, *Pesaḥim* 7.10. Neusner 1988: 243.
155. De Vaux 1965: II, 485.
156. Lev. 7.15.
157. Lev. 7.17.
158. Lev. 7.28–34.
159. 2 Chron. 7–9.
160. The Mishnah, *Pesaḥim* 5.2. Neusner 1988: 237.
161. The Mishnah, *Pesaḥim* 5.2. Neusner 1988: 237.
162. Philo, *Spec. Leg.* I, 168–295.
163. Exod. 12.21; 2 Chron. 30.15, 17; 35.1, 6, 11; Ezra 6.20.
164. 2 Chron. 35.13.

that before the ritual became a national obligation the Passover sacrifice consisted of only one animal which was collectively eaten. In any case, the distinctiveness that in every respect surrounds it is a very strong signal that the animal that was killed and eaten as part of the ritual was not even a sacrifice in the traditional sense of an offering to a god.

The particular manner in which the ritual is organized demonstrates that its function was far more complex and far more different than that of a mere commemoration. The restrictions imposed on its time, space and participants indicate that the ritual involved separation, transition and incorporation, which are conditions and stages typical for rites of passage.[165] The separation was obviously effected by entering the temple, or any other enclosed space where the flesh of the sacrificial animal was to be eaten. The perimeters of the enclosure marked the exclusion zone within which the rite was allowed to be performed. The time markers of the separation were the setting of the sun and the arrival of the dawn. The transitional stage took place between those two markers, that is to say, during night-time proper. The morning brought into effect the third stage, the reincorporation of the participants into the community. In different rites of passage the distribution of acts performed as part of each of the three stages greatly varies. In some cases, the majority of ritual acts are carried out as part of the separation, while in others the focus might be on transition or reincorporation.[166] In the case of the Passover ritual the accent is obviously on transition given that the main acts regarding the sacrificial animal, the eating of its flesh and the burning of the remains, occur during this stage.

The function of being a rite of passage provides the necessary general framework within which, as was said earlier, it is possible to attempt the interpretation of the ritual on the first night of Passover. However, given that the emphasis of the ritual itself is on transition it is necessary to give a short explanation of the nature of this particular sequence and the role it plays in every rite of passage.

The transitional phase is the most important moment in every rite of passage because it gives the rite its creative, transformative powers. It allows the otherwise very clear boundaries that divide structure and anti-structure, order and chaos, culture and nature to become blurred and indistinguishable. By symbolically obliterating the established and the structured,[167] the transitional phase allows the creation of new and different orders and forms. Its character of 'betwixt and between' also

---

165.   D. Bergant also comes to the conclusion that the ritual has the character of a rite of passage, but accepts the classical interpretation that it is of nomadic origin and that it deals with transition to new grazing grounds. Bergant 1995: 53.

166.   Van Gennep 1960: 10–11.

167.   Turner 1974: 253; 1979: 166–203.

permits relaxation or abeyance of social rules, restrictions and cultural taboos. Freedom from such constraints, on the other hand, means that during this stage participants are free to perform acts that represent or are indeed violation of taboos, transgression of the moral code and conventional social behaviour. Exactly by permitting the impermissible the transitional stage generates a change, a movement, a transformation.

As will be seen, it is specifically this context of 'betwixt and between', of being allowed to generate a change through destruction, that will make the meaning of certain elements of the ritual during the first night understandable.

3.3.2. *The Vigil*

As already mentioned, one of the elements of the ritual was an all-night vigil and we have discussed its connotations of danger and crisis in relation to night as the time when the eating of the sacrificial animal was performed. In this section, however, we shall investigate the meaning of vigil as a form of ritual behaviour.

According to Exod. 12.42 the first night of Passover is a night of watching: 'It was a night of the watching by the Lord, to bring them out of the land of Egypt; so this same night is a watching kept to the Lord by all the people of Israel throughout their generations.' Although the Bible would have us believe that the vigil during Passover ritual meant nothing more than a way of paying homage and showing gratitude for the actions of Yahweh, vigils immanently and in practice, in particular when they are part of structured actions as is the case with rituals, mean more than just merely staying awake at night. Job tosses and turns all night, but his wakefulness is not a vigil.[168] Neither is the nightly meditation of the Psalmist.[169] With these two examples, vigils share the quality of being a departure from man's everyday rhythm of active and inactive periods, but are nevertheless also fundamentally different from them. In contrast to Job's forced wakefulness, vigils are characterized by an intention, by a conscious choice to be awake. David's vigil, for example, lasts as long as his child is alive and he cannot be persuaded to cease it earlier.[170] In contrast to the Psalmist's intentional, but essentially passive wakefulness,

168. Job 7.4: When I lie down I say, 'When shall I arise?' But the night is long, and I am full of tossing till the dawn.

169. Ps. 119.148: My eyes are awake before the watches of the night, that I may meditate upon thy promise.

170. 2 Sam. 12.16–23. (16) David therefore besought God for the child; and David fasted, and went in and lay all night upon the ground. (17) And the elders of his house stood beside him, to raise him from the ground; but he would not, nor did he eat food with them. (18) On the seventh day the child died. And the servants of David feared to tell him that the child was dead; for they said, 'Behold, while the child was yet alive, we spoke to him, and he did not listen to us; how then can we say to him the child is dead? He may do himself some harm.'

vigils are dynamic affairs that require and usually involve a certain course of action. David's vigil, for example, involves praying, fasting and laying on the ground. Regardless of the form that it actually might have, whether it is a simple prayer or something more complicated, the performed activity, as we learn from David's example, has a very clear and specific purpose. It aims to influence the force that is otherwise perceived to be beyond man's control to move into a direction that is beneficial from the point of view of the person carrying out the vigil.

Generally speaking, as an intentional behaviour, vigils represent defiance to submit to the compelling force of the natural day/night cycle. In this sense they symbolize a conscious and organized attempt on behalf of people to break away from dependence on forces perceived to be superior to man and the passive acceptance of the subordinate role implicit in that relationship. Activities that are performed as part of vigils are a form of resisting the superiority of such forces and not surrendering to their potential volatility. They are an attempt at exercising a control over what is perceived as essentially transcendent and ungovernable and as such also potentially detrimental for interests idiosyncratic to man. The night, with its mysteriousness and close connections with the chaotic elements, as was pointed out earlier, epitomizes the character of such forces.

Vigils are a way of contact between the unknown and the known, the divine and the human, the nature and culture. They are an intentional overstepping of the boundaries of the world immanent to man, culture, and therefore also an intrusion of that world into the domain of what is comprehended as transcendent. As such they are a dangerous activity undertaken only in situations that are seen as ultimately critical and perilous for the interests of humans.

Given that Passover as a festival took place during an enormously important and critical period of the year, the forces that the Israelites tried to influence and control were obviously the forces of nature on which the success of the harvest depended. The compulsory vigil on the first night of Passover was a conscious and deliberate attempt by the Israelites to reign those forces and impose on the world of nature their own will and view of

(19) But when David saw that his servants were whispering together, David perceived that the child was dead; and David said to his servants, 'Is the child dead?' They said, 'He is dead.' (20) Then David arose from the earth, and washed, and anointed himself, and changed his clothes; and he went into the house of the LORD, and worshipped; he then went to his own house; and when he asked, they set food before him, and he ate. (21) Then his servants said to him, 'What is this thing that you have done? You fasted and wept for the child while it was alive; but when the child died, you arose and ate food.' (22) He said, 'While the child was still alive, I fasted and wept; for I said, "Who knows whether the LORD will be gracious to me, that the child may live?" (23) But now he is dead; why should I fast? Can I bring him back again? I shall go to him, but he will not return to me.'

order.[171] This symbolic imposition of the world of culture onto nature was expressed not only through the night vigil, but was articulated through many other details of the rite itself.

The ritual was performed in an enclosed space, which is a symbol of culture because only people build shelters that can almost completely protect them from the whims of nature. Enclosed space is an ordered space that stands in opposition to the openness of the wilderness.[172] It is the symbolic space of culture in which the close encounter between the people and the forces of nature takes place. One might argue that during Tabernacles we have a similar situation because of the huts which were built and in which people dwelled during the festival. But in the case of this festival we do not have the compulsory vigil as a symbol of the human world attempting to impose its will on nature. During Tabernacles we have the presence of culture, but within the context of nature. Huts are only temporary shelters, quickly built and quickly dismantled, and the ritual space where the majority of acts were performed was shared between the temple courts and the open fields. During Tabernacles the culture and nature work in unison, complementing each other. During the first night of Passover they stand in opposition.

The restriction to men as participants in the Passover ritual, which was discussed above as possible in times before the Yahwistic changes, is also a symbolic representation of involvement of culture and its ordering character. Because of the mystery that surrounds conception, pregnancy and birth, women are seen as closer to the equally unfathomable sphere of nature in comparison to men.[173] In the story of Eden, the woman's submission to the overtures of the chaotic forces, the snake, is the reason why people are expelled from the garden, the idealized projection of perfectly ordered and disciplined nature.[174] In coercing nature during the Passover night vigil into a desirable direction from the human perspective, only men, the symbolic deputies of culture, are involved. In contrast, during Tabernacles both women and men participate in the rituals. At one stage, women and men exchange their places in the courtyard symbolically representing the season in which nature takes over the rule.[175] The

171. In line with the vigil's symbolism of control is the uniformity of participants' clothes which does not just signal belonging to a particular group, but also subscription to and enforcement of particular values and goals. Group membership visibly expressed by wearing the same clothes is always associated with control and power. Joseph 1986: 65–83. On the numerous meanings of wearing particular clothes see Roach and Eicher 1979: 7–21.

172. In Num. 20.4–5 wilderness is described as an 'evil place'. As a spatial category it is a space of the untamed and therefore also of the chaotic or potentially chaotic forces. Talmon 1976: 946–48; Cohn 1981: 7–23.

173. Campbell 1991: 59–60.

174. Gen. 3.1–19.

175. The Mishnah, *Sukkah* 5.2. Neusner 1988: 288.

Passover request for circumcized men only further highlights this symbolism of culture intruding into the world of nature because such men are not symbolic of just any fertile men, but of men who owe their maximized fertility to a cultural intervention. They bear the imprints of culture on what came from nature, on their bodies.

The vigil's function as a deliberate attempt to influence natural forces into a desirable direction from the human perspective adds a special twist to the passage function of Passover's first-night ritual. As was said earlier, rites of passage have the power to transform, and in ordinary rites of passage that transformation is most often intended for the rite's participants. Passover's ritual in this respect was a special kind of rite of passage because the expected transformation was not aimed at the participants, but obviously at the natural force which the Israelites wanted to control at this particular time of the year. Within this context, the main questions are what particular natural force were they trying to influence and what was the meaning of the acts that were performed in order to effect the expected transformation, questions that bring the act of eating, the sacrificial animal and the removal of its remains and their symbolic references into the foreground of our discussion.

3.3.3. *The Eating*
To start on the path of interpreting correctly the meaning of the particular acts performed during the night of vigil, the eating of the sacrificial animal and the removal of its remains, it is necessary to recall that they were performed as part of the transitional phase of the ritual. We also have to recall that activities performed during this particular stage are very often a transgression of what is culturally permissible or a taboo violation and while permitted for the participants, they are forbidden in ordinary, non-ritual times and for people who do not take part in the rite.

From this angle, eating of the Passover sacrifice appears as a kind of taboo violation, which might sound bizarre because eating is one of the basic necessities and as such it is hardly ever culturally sanctioned in any fundamental way. Given also that none of the animals used as paschal sacrifices were the subject of some particular dietary taboo, the claim that the ritual eating could represent in some sense a violation of the moral code or a taboo sounds even more eccentric.

However, the situation changes when we consider the symbolic references of eating. Most often and most naturally, as an act that is vital in satisfying the basic need of every living creature, the need for nourishment, eating has positive symbolic references and means life or subsistence of life. However, it has an ominous side as well since it means a physical disappearance of the thing that is eaten. From the perspective of the eater, eating means life; from the perspective of the eaten it means material destruction, disappearance or ultimately death. The eater is always a destroyer. Samson's riddle seems unsolvable exactly because it plays with the contradictory symbolism of eating.[176] From the lion, the eater, or in other words from something that removes, eliminates life, comes the honey, something to be eaten and something that sustains life.

The Bible preserves both meanings, although most frequently the term 'eating' emphasizes its positive side. In the couple of examples in which it is used in its negative aspect, 'eating' is a metaphor for ruin or death. The Psalimst says that evildoers eat up people like bread.[177] In the Proverbs, a disrespectful child will be picked by ravens and eaten by vultures.[178]

More often the threatening aspect of eating is expressed by terms such as 'devouring' and 'swallowing'. Fire,[179] wild beasts,[180] swords,[181] locusts,[182] flies,[183] alien nations[184] and generally destructive and uncontrollable forces of any kind, including Yahweh in his anger, devour. In contrast to 'devouring' which always implies a very messy death, 'swallowing' resonates with more orderly elimination because it means a disappearance rather than a destruction. In the pharaoh's dream the thin ears swallow the plump and full ones, making them disappear.[185] The same is the case with Aaron's rod which swallows the rods of other people.[186] And, as a punishment, Yahweh makes people vanish by making the earth swallow them.[187]

Death and the abode of the dead, Sheol, are also closely associated with the idea of eating. In Isa. 5.14 we read: 'Therefore Sheol has enlarged its appetite and opened its mouth beyond measure.' A similar picture appears in the Proverbs: 'like Sheol let us swallow them alive and whole'.[188] Eating and the symbolism of death go hand in hand and it is obvious that the consumption of the sacrificial animal during the first night of Passover could have been performed in its negative aspect. From this perspective, the ritual that the Israelites perform during the night of exodus looks like nothing more than a disguised imitation of Yahweh's killing mission. However, given that all of the flesh of the animal was required to be eaten

---

176. Judg. 14.14. 'Out of the eater came something to eat.'
177. Ps. 14.4.
178. Prov. 30.17.
179. Lev. 10.2; Num. 26.10.
180. Isa. 56.9.
181. 2 Sam. 2.26; 11.25.
182. 2 Chron. 7.13.
183. Ps. 78.45.
184. Isa. 1.7.
185. Gen. 41.7.
186. Exod. 7.12.
187. Num. 16.32.
188. Prov. 1.12.

while its remains were to be burned, the negative implication of the ritual seems to have had more the form of a disappearance, symbolic removal or in biblical terms 'swallowing' than destruction or 'devouring'.[189]

There is more indirect evidence that Passover as a festival had some connections with death and related concepts. In the biblical texts it is never described as a very relaxed or particularly joyful festival which somehow contradicts its declared purpose given that the event it allegedly commemorates, a release from slavery, certainly provides a very good reason for genuine jubilance. In Deuteronomy, which is the only legislation that hints at the atmosphere that prevailed at individual festivals, the feasts that are described as joyful are the Weeks[190] and the Tabernacle.[191] In both cases the people are specially called to rejoice before Yahweh. Passover is the only one among the three feasts of the cultic cycle for which Deuteronomy is silent in this respect. Neither is any of the reported celebration described as particularly joyful except for Passovers of Hezekiah[192] and the returned exiles,[193] but the reason for joy during those festivals had to do more with the alleged historical circumstances than with Passover itself. In contrast to Weeks and Tabernacles it seems that, regarding public display of sentiments, Passover was imbued with a very subdued atmosphere. Philo saw it as a very solemn occasion and urged the people not to indulge in excessive drinking and feasting.[194] It seems that the subdued atmosphere continued until Weeks, that is during the whole period of harvest or the sheaves counting (omer). Even today the days of omer are a period of sadness and half mourning during which merriment, the first haircuts, celebration of marriages and wearing of new clothes are forbidden. The only reason for this behaviour is a vague statement in the Talmud that tells of 12,000 pairs of Rabbi Akiba's disciples that were allegedly killed by plague during the period of omer counting.[195]

However, having Passover as a not particularly happy festival or showing that eating in general as a symbol has an ominous side does not demonstrate that the ritual eating during the first night of Passover was in any sense a taboo violation, a claim we made at the beginning of this chapter. To prove this last point and, therefore, also to demonstrate that

---

189. In psychology, the act of eating can mean control by incorporation. Such control can be exercized over things that are desired, but also over things that are seen as negative and unwanted. From a private communication with Stojanka Stefanovic, clinical psychologist.
190. Deut. 16.11.
191. Deut. 16.14.
192. 2 Chron. 30.25–26.
193. Ezra 6.22.
194. Philo, *Spec. Leg.* II, 147–48.
195. Werbulowsky and Wigoder 1967: 290.

the eating was intentionally employed in its negative aspect we have to refer to the Mishnah and its description of the unusual behaviour in which people engaged while consuming the flesh of the sacrificial animal. The description refers to the performance of the ritual in the times when everyone was obliged to participate in it and when it was centralized to the Jerusalem temple. These two developments, as was said earlier, forced some changes, so there were many groups and some of them had to share the space where they performed the ritual eating. According to the Mishnah, in such situations the groups had to eat with their heads turned away from the group to which they did not belong. The person who prepared the wine and in that capacity served everyone who took part in the ritual, but was actually eating together with the members of only one of the groups, had to mix and pour the wine for those who were not members of his own group also with his head turned away from them and furthermore with his mouth closed. In other words, he had to temporarily stop chewing. He was allowed to resume eating once he went back among the members of his own group.[196]

The Mishnah does not give any reasons for this very strange behaviour. What is, however, clear from the posture that the people tried to maintain with respect to the other group, that is to have their faces turned away, and particularly from the waiter's suspension of eating while serving the people who did not belong to his own association, is that groups tried to conceal from each other the mastication movements or, in other words, the act of eating.

Intentional attempts to conceal some activity from others always imply that there is something objectionable about it. However, in order to understand how an act could have been perceived as objectionable or as breaking a taboo while at the same time being performed by every single person present in the room, we have to recall that before its centralization and the introduction of a national context the performance of the rite was restricted to one place and to one group of people. Everyone that was outside the spatial-group (and time) confines was excluded. The rite was allowed only to the group that was inside the designated space and only during the allotted time.[197] However, with the above-mentioned changes,

---

196. The Mishnah, *Pesahim* 7.13. A. Two associations [registered for two separate Passover offerings] which were eating in one room – B. these turn their faces to one side and eat, C. and those turn their faces to the other side and eat. D. And the kettle is in the middle [between them]. E. And when the waiter [who eats with one association but serves them both] stands up to mix the wine [of the company with which he is not eating] F. he shuts his mouth and turns his face away until he gets back to his own association, G. and then continues eating. Neusner 1988: 244.

197. In Van Gennep's examination of rites of passage associated with dying and death in general the most prominent and most elaborate stage, like in Passover's first-night ritual, is the stage of transition. Van Gennep 1960: 146.

people had to form many groups and needless to say some of them had to share the space where they would perform the rite. On the other hand, its character as a taboo violation, or doing something that is for people outside the designated group not just forbidden, but also not acceptable as well, was preserved. So, in a sense, everyone who shared the same space while eating was both permitted and banned from performing the act. Permitted within their own group, but forbidden from the perspective of the other group. Subsequently, each group behaved in a manner that befits those who are intent on violating taboo, committing a sin and generally doing something that oversteps the boundaries of established cultural values and norms. They tried to hide their actions from those who might object to them – in other words, the other group.[198]

This discussion of taboo breaking during the transitional stage of the ritual brings us to the question of the meaning of the sacrificial animals. For eating to be performed as an act of elimination and at the same time to be a step beyond the permitted, it is obvious that the consumed animal had to represent something which in non-ritual circumstances was a taboo or whose life was a taboo. In the next section we shall try to find an answer to the questions of who or what was represented by the animals whose flesh was eaten and who or what was subjected to the symbolic removal.

3.3.4. *The Sacrificial Animal*
When the symbolic removal that was performed through eating is placed in perspective with everything else that we said about the symbolic references of Passover – namely, the meaning of the season, the first night as a paradigm of the chaotic forces, the vigil as an attempt to control powers that are otherwise beyond human reach – it becomes clear that the objective of the ritual on the first night was essentially the elimination of the natural force that was seen as undesirable at that specific time of the year, that is at the time of the harvest. The animals that were eaten obviously represented that force. The answer to the question which particular aspect of nature concerned the Israelites at this point of the year, however, cannot be found in the Bible, which by choosing this rite to be central for the Yahwistic ideology replaced its references to the harvest and natural forces with their historicized versions. To find that answer we have to turn to the traditions of Ugarit and one of its myths, the myth about Mot and Baal. The primary reason for referring to this myth is because there are so many parallels between the ideas it employs and the circumstances of Passover that it is clear that both originated from a

---

198.   According to the Mishnah, another breach of rules was attempted to be concealed. Women had to keep their heads turned away and conceal their eating all the time, irrespective of the group, which only confirms that the original participants were males. The Mishnah, *Pesahim* 7.13. Neusner 1988: 244.

shared cultural tradition. For the purpose of this work the myth is enlightening because it reveals the natural force that the Israelites tried to control through eating.

The myth deals with the encounter between Mot, a personified death[199] and Baal, the rain god. The myth, however, is not an independent unit and comes as a continuation of another one in which Baal defeats Yam, the sea, and builds a palace. After completing its construction, Baal very ostentatiously declares that he is the king over gods and people because they all depend on him for their food.[200] In his pretentiousness, he decides to challenge even death itself, Mot, and dispatches messengers to him. At this point begins the unfolding of events that are of direct interest for us. Mot is described as a voracious eater whose lip reaches to the sky and who has an insatiable appetite. Baal is the ruler over rains, winds, thunderbolts and clouds and is the lord of the earth.[201] Throughout the myth, the narrator refers to the death that will come to Baal when he encounters Mot through descriptions that involve eating. Baal will 'go down into the throat of divine Mot' and 'Baal must enter his innards and go down into his mouth'. It is unclear how Baal actually dies, but he is discovered dead and his sister Anath gives him a proper burial. Grieving for her brother, Anath finds Mot who tells her how Baal died. 'I it was who confronted mightiest Baal, I who made him a lamb in my mouth, he was carried away like a kid in the breach of my windpipe.'[202] After Anath kills Mot in a manner that very much resembles the activities performed during harvest, El, the head god, dreams that Baal is alive and the sun goddess Shapash is dispatched to find him because the earth is dry and parched. What happens afterwards and how the rain god really comes to life we do not know because the inscription is at that particular point destroyed. But, where it continues it is obvious that Baal is truly alive because he is engaged in a battle with some kind of henchmen of Mot's and Mot himself who apparently also recovered from his own death.

It is obvious that there are many parallels in the way in which the death of the rain god was represented in this myth and the ideas that are related to Passover. In both of them, eating appears as an act with close connections to death. Then there are the animals with which Mot compares Baal's weakness and which were also the main kinds of animals eaten during the first night of Passover, namely lambs and kids. And finally there is the parallel between the aspect in which Baal dies, as the rain god, and the season in which Passover takes place, that is at the beginning of the harvest season when the rains are expected to cease and are actually

199. Mot means death.
200. Gibson 1978: 66.
201. Gibson 1978: 72.
202. Gibson 1978.

undesirable. These similarities are a strong indication that the ritual eating of the Passover animal was aimed at ending the season of rains and that the object of the symbolic removal through eating was the rain god. The uniqueness of the Passover sacrifice that has already been discussed certainly supports this view, in particular the singular form of the expression used to designate the animals that were consumed despite their actual numbers and heterogeneity. If they were supposed to represent the rains in their personified form as the rain god, it is no wonder that all of them were referred to as being one, 'the passover lamb'. From this perspective it also becomes clear that it was the rain god who was the focus of the passage function of the ritual and that it was him who was expected to come out of it transformed. Perhaps dead, or only absent or dormant, but in any case incapacitated to produce 'rains, winds, thunderbolts and clouds' during harvest. On the other hand, participation or aiding in the demise of a deity could certainly be comprehended as performing an otherwise tabooed activity since divine beings and their lives are for people intrinsically sacrosanct.[203] In this context one cannot escape wondering whether the participation in the removal of the rain god was the reason why Isaiah accused the Jerusalemites of making a covenant with death and Sheol.[204] Even more so, given that he threatens them with Yahweh's revenge in his aspect as a rain god, by hail and sweeping waters.[205]

Most often the Ugaritic myth is explained as a representation of the autumnal change of seasons, summer being symbolic of Baal's death and autumn of his revival,[206] and it is possible to argue that it is wrong to use it as a source of parallels for a festival that takes place in spring. However, as in the case of Gaster's interpretation of the meaning of the sun, the

203. Perhaps additional support for the divine qualities of the Passover animal can be found in wearing the special clothes that is stipulated in the book of Exodus 12.11. The act of clothing as such has many functions that can be translated into a variety of symbolical meanings. One of them is that it is a kind of putting on of a disguise, a mask that protects the true identity of the person wearing it. From this perspective it is possible to argue that the special outfit worn during the first night of Passover was not solely a sign of particular membership as was said before, but a real disguise or a costume with the purpose of shielding the participants in the ritual from recognition by the rain god whose wrath they certainly wanted to avoid, but in whose mortification they nevertheless actively participated. According to Joseph, wearing a costume means 'open declaration of departure in behaviour', in our case a performance of tabooed activity. Joseph 1986: 184.

204. Isa. 28.14–15a. (14) Therefore hear the word of the LORD, you scoffers, who rule this people in Jerusalem! (15) Because you have said, 'We have made a covenant with death, and with Sheol we have an agreement;

205. Isa. 28.17: And I will make justice the line, and righteousness the plummet; and hail will sweep away the refuge of lies, and waters will overwhelm the shelter.

206. Gibson 1978: 77. De Moor 1972: I, 5. One of the few exceptions to this interpretation is Mark S. Smith's view that 'Baal's death reflects the demise of Ugaritic kings, but his return to life heralds the role of the living king to provide peace for the world.' Smith 2001: 128.

aforementioned explanation also rests on a very one-dimensional understanding of rain that places an overwhelming importance on its fertilizing
powers, but disregards the fact that rain, as any other natural phenomenon, has its negative aspect as well. In its background is also a very
restrictive conception of the nature of seasonal myths that instead of
considering the myth's overall dynamics concentrates only on one of its
points, most often the one that can be interpreted as a focus in a potential
ritual situation.[207] However, myths that deal with phenomena which
appear in more or less regular cycles, such as the verdure or rains, are
usually an explanation of the cycle as a whole and not just of one of its
parts. The point is that as much as the myth about Baal and Mot is a
representation of the autumnal revival of rains and can be for that matter
connected with Tabernacles, it is equally a representation of their spring
cessation and therefore can be a fruitful source of parallels for Passover. It
is important to recognize that some myths involving deities embodying
natural cyclic phenomena were actually celebrated more than once a year.
The Greek Eleusinian mysteries were held twice a year, in spring and
autumn. According to Frazer, it is likely that there was more than one
festival dedicated to Adonis, the Phoenician version of the reviving god.[208]
Blackman claims that in Egypt the majority of the great annual festivals
were also in some respect associated with the myth of Osiris' death and
revival.[209] Finally, Mettinger's analysis of a range of Near Eastern dying
and resurrecting gods also comes up with more than one festival in the
case of Dumuzi, Adonis, Melqart and Osiris.[210] The purpose of all these
seasonal myths was not merely to be an explanation, but indeed a
corroboration of the changes in question, of establishing an equilibrium
between the necessity for the appearance of the phenomenon at a
particular time of the year and the necessity of its absence at another
period of the year. Seasonal rituals, regardless of whether they are
associated with some myth or not, were the practical endorsement of the
changes in question and the necessary equilibrium.

207.   The most illustrative example is James's interpretation of the Baal/Mot myth. James
1961: 92–98.
208.   Frazer 1914: 223–26.
209.   Blackman 1933: 15.
210.   Mettinger 2001: 219–20. The mentioned examples, which clearly demonstrate that in
terms of dates essentially the same mythological motif was represented in more than one
point in time during the natural year, are perhaps an indication that the similarities that exist
between Passover and Tabernacles both in view of their ritual characteristics and their
functions may have resulted from the same theme that the two festivals shared as their
mythological framework. It is interesting to note that Tawil argues that Azazel, a demonic
figure for whom a goat was sent on the Day of Atonement, is Mot in disguise, the god of
death and all evil. He claims that the name Azazel means 'a fierce god', a description which is
used for Mot. Tawil 1980: 58–59.

With respect to rains the desired regularity of changes is mainly connected with and refers to the world of plants and the necessity for water during different phases in their development. In the circumstances of the ancient Near East the benefit of rains was measured against the need for water during different stages in the growth of cereals given that they were the main source of food for the majority of people. From the agrarian perspective, rains are indeed crucial in autumn and winter in order to soften the soil so that it can be ploughed, then for germination of the seeds and the growth of stalks and development of the ears of grain. However, once the ears are fully formed and the grains become 'milky' while the only thing remaining before the actual harvest is the drying or hardening of the grains, wet weather can come only as a punishment and a curse. As was pointed out earlier, the time immediately before harvest is the hungriest period during the whole year and although milky grains can be eaten parched, which might bring temporary relief, they do not altogether remove the threat of starvation because they cannot be stored in order to be used until the next harvest. For the grains to reach the stage at which they can be safely stored to last for the rest of the year, sun and dry weather are vital.

There are many reasons why rains and wet conditions in general are in this particular period harmful. One of them is that excessive moisture prevents the ears from ripening and the grains rot if they are exposed to such conditions for a longer period. In the Mishnah, for example, rains after the month of Nissan, the month of Passover, are considered as a sign of curse.[211] Too much water at this stage can also be a cause for the appearance of mildew and similar fungal diseases of the crops which thrive in damp conditions and can destroy the whole harvest. In the Bible their destructive powers are equal to those of drought, locusts, caterpillars and hail.[212] According to the Mishnah, the appearance of blasting or mildew the size of an 'oven's mouth' was enough to sound the shofar in every community because they are 'infliction that spreads'.[213] In this context it becomes clear that the removal and destruction of leaven at the time of Passover and the use of unleavened bread during the seven days of festival were simple homeopathic acts in order to protect the new crops from decay that can come from excessive water. Leaven was destroyed and avoided because it was basically a mixture of water and flour, a fermented lump of yesterday's dough. In this sense, since fermentation is also a kind of putrefaction, leaven is also a kind of 'infliction that spreads'. Given that it is the contact with water that causes fermentation, it is clear that using unleavened bread meant primarily avoidance of

211.   The Mishnah, *Taanit* 1.7.VI.D. Neusner 1988: 308.
212.   Deut. 28.22; 1 Kgs 8.37; 2 Chron. 6.28; Amos 4.9; Hag. 2.17.
213.   The Mishnah, *Taanit* 3.5.B. Neusner 1988: 312.

water's corrupting abilities. Even today, the so-called 'watched unleavened bread' basically means special care over the wheat right from the time it is harvested in order to prevent its contact with water. Both the removal of the leaven and the use of the unleavened bread imply prevention of consequences that water and wet weather can inflict on the crops.

There are some indications that the avoidance of water was also present in the preparation of the flesh of the paschal sacrifice. In Exod. 12.9 it is stipulated that it is not to be eaten raw or boiled in water. R.J. Smith raized the question of the purpose of the ban on consuming raw flesh, but little attention has been paid to the second part of the prohibition in which boiling in water is banned.[214] Most frequently it is held that the main concern of the regulation is to uphold roasting as the original way of preparing the flesh for consumption. However, one cannot escape wondering why it was necessary specifically to mention water as the liquid in which the flesh of the animal must not be cooked if the author of this regulation wanted to forbid boiling in general? The point is, was he trying to ensure the prevention of boiling as a way of preparation or was he trying to prevent contact between water in particular and the flesh? In Deut. 16.7, for example, it is boiling that is the required way of preparation. It is habitually taken that this means boiling in water, but the regulation actually does not specify the kind of liquid that is to be used. Was there any other liquid that was used for cooking meat and which in the case of the Passover sacrifice could have been used as a water substitute? Such a notion would not just explain the emphasis of the Exodus ban on boiling in water without, on the other hand, contradicting the Deuteronomic rule, but would also support the thesis that avoidance of water was one of the characteristics of Passover in general. Perhaps milk, which is mentioned in the ban on boiling a kid in his mother's milk in Exod. 34.26, was the other liquid in which meat could be cooked. This rule is usually discussed for other reasons, such as the meaning of the prohibition,[215] but in the context of our claim that water was avoided because of its corrupting abilities it demonstrates that water was not the only choice for boiling meat. If Passover animal or some of its parts were boiled,[216] it could have been done in milk instead of water.[217]

214. Smith 1907: 345.

215. This very strange ban was later interpreted and transformed into a halakhic rule as a prohibition on mixing milk and meat, but it seems that it actually deals with prohibiting killing very young animals, that is animals that still suckle, which is designated by the phrase 'in his mother's milk' which succinctly suggests the maturity of the animal.

216. 2 Chron. 35.13 mentions that parts of the flesh were boiled.

217. Perhaps boiling in milk was not just a way to avoid the putrefying capacity of water with respect to the body of the rain god, but also because milk was comprehended to be in some way connected with the milky stage of the crops.

Abundant rains and wet conditions mean promise of life in autumn; however, in the period that immediately precedes the harvest and during harvest time[218] when that promise should become reality, they can mean starvation. From the human perspective, rains can be both a blessing and a curse.[219] Whether they will be symbolic of life and will have fertilizing powers or whether they will be an unruly and unpredictable destructive force symbolic of chaos depends on whether they appear and vanish in regular cycles and that idea is clearly expressed in the Bible. Giving rain in its 'due season' is one of the ways in which Yahweh's blessing is demonstrated.[220] When Jeremiah describes the powers of Yahweh he refers to giving rain in its season and keeping the weeks of harvest as an appointed time, which quite clearly demonstrates that rains stand in an antagonistic relationship with the harvest.[221]

Following the usual cycle of seasonal change means that rains belong to the cosmos, the world of order.[222] Disruption or deviation in that cycle transforms them into a chaotic, threatening and possibly destructive force, in particular when that happens during the period of harvest that was from the Israelite perspective, as we have seen, the ultimate expression of cosmic order.[223] In the Sephardic tradition, on the first day of the festival a prayer for dew is recited signifying that the period of rains is over. In contrast, in autumn, during Tabernacles a prayer for rain takes place. The two prayers that symmetrically divide the year into two seasons, one of dew and one of rain, one prayer marking the time of the harvest, the other the time of ploughing, demonstrate that, while both dew and rain were symbols of fertility and life, their importance and desirability changed

218.   In Prov. 26.1 the inappropriateness of rain in harvest is equated with that of honour for a foolish person.

219.   In the apocryphal book of Ezra both a lack of rain in its due season, but also too much of it are specified as causes for destruction of the crops. 4 Ezra 8.43.

220.   Lev. 26.4; Deut. 11.14; 28.12.

221.   Jer. 5.24.

222.   In the Ugaritic tradition, only when Baal builds his palace, a symbolic rendition of rains as a seasonal phenomenon, does he become equal to other gods that represent the world of cosmic order. This is clear from the words that the goddess Athirat addresses to El, the head god, after he approves the construction of the palace: 'Now at last, Baal may appoint a time for his rain, a time for (his) barque (to appear) in the snow and for the sounding of his voice in the clouds, for him to release (his) lightnings on the earth.' Gibson 1978: 60. In contrast to the myth about Baal's encounter with Mot where he already represents rains as a cyclic phenomenon and in which he gets defeated, in the palace-building myth Baal personifies rains as a paradigm of fresh waters and their fertilizing powers that stand in opposition to the infertile, salty waters of the sea, Yam. This palace-building tradition as an expression of the rains as part of the world of order on the other hand perhaps explains why the first festival held in the temple that Solomon built for Yahweh was the autumnal Tabernacles rather than the spring Passover.

223.   See section 3.2.1, 'The Season'.

with the agricultural seasons. In spring, during harvest, dew takes over the role as the life-giving power.

Making the rain god inactive through performing the ritual on Passover's first night was, similar to the removal of leaven, a preventative measure against his destructive side. This explains why the ceremonial reaping of the first sheaf of barley and its presentation in the temple had to wait until the second night, although the preparations for it were carried out on the afternoon of the first day of the festival.[224] Obviously, the harvesting could begin only after effectively removing the threat that prolonged rains could pose at this particular point of the year.

Apart from only circumstantial evidence, such as we have presented, no trace of the rain god's connection with the first night of Passover has been preserved in the Bible.[225] However, in post-temple times he again found his way into the festival, disguized as Elijah, the prophet whose main miracle was to produce rain, who did not die, but was taken to heaven in a blazing chariot, a symbol of the sun. During Seder there is always a cup of wine set aside for him.

Like Elijah, the rain god was also expected to return. The idea of return brings us to the final components of the first-night ritual, the ban on breaking the bones of the Passover animal and the removal of its remains.

3.3.5. *Treatment of the Bones*

There are several closely related aspects of the symbolism of bones. They represent the permanent, imperishable part of the body that stands in opposition to the flesh, the transient and easily destructible element that is comparable to a passing wind and dust.[226] Bones are the solid inner frame that keep together the fragile, visible exterior. According to Job 10.11, bones and sinews keep the body together while skin and flesh are like a cloth, only a covering for the frame. They are also the only element that survives the decomposition that death brings upon the body and the only trace of the life that once existed. The bones of Joseph, the patriarch who brought the predecessors of the Israelites to Egypt, are taken during the night of exodus[227] and re-buried in the promised

---

224.   The Mishnah, *Menahot* 10.3. Neusner 1988: 753–54.

225.   It is interesting to note that in the early Christian practice there were two modes of celebrating Easter. The one which ultimately became universal placed the focus on 'Christ has risen' and was celebrated on Sunday. The other, called 'Quartodecimans', followed the date of Passover and was celebrated during the night between the 14th and the 15th of Nisan. The focus of this celebration was not on resurrection, but on Christ's death, 'Christ, the passover lamb, sacrificed for us.' Bradshaw 1999: 81–97.

226.   Ps. 78.39; Job 34.15.

227.   Exod. 13.19: And Moses took the bones of Joseph with him; for Joseph had solemnly sworn the people of Israel, saying, 'God will visit you; then you must carry my bones with you from here.'

land.[228] In this sense, bones symbolize permanence, continuation and preservation of identity.

Like the spilling of blood, exposure of bones means death but, on the other hand, like blood, they also contain the essence of life and have special properties that mainly deal with creation or re-creation of life. Adam's companion Eve is fashioned from his rib.[229] In Eccl. 11.5 creation of life in a woman's womb is accomplished when spirit enters the bones of the child. By touching the bones of the prophet Elisha, a dead man comes back to life.[230] To demonstrate his powers to Ezekiel Yahweh revives very dry bones, a metaphor for death that happened a long time ago. The bones are covered with sinews, flesh and finally these remodelled bodies are filled with the breath of life.[231]

Bones are the inner, invisible core of life around which its visible manifestation, the body, is built. Their preservation in death means a possibility that life can be restored. From this perspective, even death can be bad or good. Death where the bones are scattered[232] or unburied[233] is the worst curse[234] because it relinquishes the hope of return. Broken bones, which in life mean decline of one's vitality, in death mean failure to return to one's full potential. Given the divine properties of the Passover sacrificial animal, the purpose of the ban on breaking any of its bones[235]

228. Josh. 24.32: The bones of Joseph which the people of Israel brought up from Egypt were buried at Shechem, in the portion of ground which Jacob bought from the sons of Hamor the father of Shehem for a hundred pieces of money; it became an inheritance of the descendants of Joseph.

229. Gen. 2.22.

230. 2 Kgs 13.21.

231. Ezek. 37.1–10.

232. Ps. 53.5: There they are, in great terror, in terror such as has not been! For God will scatter the bones of the ungodly; Ezek. 6.5: And I will lay the dead bodies of the people of Israel before their idols; and I will scatter your bones round about your altars. Jer. 8.1–2: (1) At that time, says the Lord, the bones of the kings of Judah, the bones of its princes, the bones of the priests, the bones of the prophets, and the bones of the inhabitants of Jerusalem shall be brought out of their tombs; (2) and they shall be spread before the sun and the moon and all the host of heaven, which they have loved and served, which they have gone after, and which they have sought and worshipped; and they shall not be gathered or buried; they shall be dung on the surface of the ground.

233. Ezek. 29.5: And I will cast you forth into the wilderness, you and the fish of your streams; you shall fall upon the open field, and not be gathered and buried. To the beasts of the earth and to the birds of the air I have given you as food. 1 Kgs 14.11: Any one belonging to Jeroboam who dies in the city the dogs shall eat; and any one who dies in the open country the birds of the air shall eat; for the Lord has spoken it.

234. Josephus Flavius mentions a mysterious incident which confirms that scattering of bones brings curse. During the night of Passover a group of Samaritans secretly scattered human bones in the porticos and the esplanade of the Jerusalem temple. Josephus does not give clear reasons as to the action of the Samaritans, but their intention is more than clear, to profane and bring curse on competition. Josephus, *Antiquities* 8.29–30.

235. Exod. 12.46; Num. 9.12.

was obviously an attempt to ensure a good death for the god, a death which will not be detrimental to his return to the world of the living and the active with all of his potency and virility. It was a precautionary measure against inadequate rains in autumn, their appointed season, since even accidental breaking could have had serious consequences.[236] Punishment awaited the person who violated the ban. What form that punishment had in times when the animal still represented the rain god, we do not know, but during the second temple, when many of the rules that governed this ritual were already relaxed, the violator had to endure forty lashes.[237]

What happened with the bones after the eating was finished? Exod. 12.10 demands burning of the remains of the animal, but it seems that the requirement refers only to the flesh since the concern of the preceding verse is the way of preparing the animals for consumption. If the bones were also burned that would have meant complete annihilation as in the case of Josiah's burning of the bones of idolatrous priests. However, such treatment would contradict the rule of not breaking them and the ideas of continuation and regeneration. The bones were the corporeal carriers of the essence of life and the god's vitality. Even if some kind of burning was involved it was probably done in order to remove the last traces of the flesh, the corruptible, failing element of the body and in a sense have the bones in a purified form. Fire destroys, but also purifies and furthermore when divine beings are involved it does not seem to have damaging effects, as the case of the burning bush demonstrates. In general, cremations originate from the human wish to control the circumstances of death since they enable a control of the natural process of decay through its acceleration.[238] Furthermore, as Hertz observed, 'cremation . . . calls for a latter and complementary rite'.[239]

The only indication of what possibly happened to the bones after the eating was over and the remains of the flesh were destroyed, comes from the story about the killing of the seven descendants of Saul.[240] The narrative begins with David seeking an answer from the Lord regarding the cause of the three-year famine. He is told that the famine is a result of the blood guilt that is on Saul and his descendants because of a broken promise given to the Gibeonites. On hearing this, David calls the Gibeonites and asks them what kind of expiation they want. Refusing money compensation, they demand the lives of seven descendants of Saul, which are to be hung before the Lord on his mountain. David agrees and

---

236. According to Bloch and Perry, 'good death' not only promises a rebirth for the individual, but also renewal of the world of living; while 'bad' death represents the loss of regenerative potential. Bloch and Perry 1982: 15–18.

237. The Mishnah, *Pesaḥim* 7.11.C. Neusner 1988: 243.

238. Davies 1997: 77.

239. Hertz 1960: 42.

240. 2 Sam. 21.

the seven perish together. Their death happens quite significantly 'in the first days of harvest, at the beginning of barley harvest'. The story continues with Rizpah, the mother of two of the killed, who goes to the place of the ritual murder, preventing birds during the day and wild beasts during the night from approaching the corpses. She stays there from the beginning of the harvest until the rains begin. When David hears about this, he gathers the bones of the killed and gives them a proper burial. Only then does the Lord give relief from the famine.

There are some obvious parallels between this story and the circumstances of Passover. First among them is the idea of famine which in the story is a reality, while in Passover it is an underlying notion with respect to the time of the year. Next, both in the story and in Passover, famine is attempted to be relived by a ritual death that is performed at the beginning of the barley harvest. And finally there is the special treatment of the bones since Rizpah's aim is obviously not to allow the wild animals to scatter or damage them. However, in contrast to Passover, where the relief from hunger can be expected without delay because the harvest is about to begin, in the story about the seven descendants of Saul, although the harvest is mentioned, the land retrieves its fertility only after the bones of the killed have been preserved from destruction and after they have been given a proper burial. What the story of the ritual killing of the seven teaches is that bones that are not subject to proper funeral ceremonies, even if the required sacrifice is made, bring curse and infertility upon the land.

Although not directly as in the story about Saul's progenies, the same idea that connects observance of proper funeral and mourning rites with fertility can be found in the Ugaritic tradition, in the already mentioned Baal/Mot myth and the myth about the death of Aqhat. In the Baal/Mot version, the revival of the rain god and his fertilizing powers happens only after Anath finds Baal's body and ceremonially buries it. Regarding the Aqhat myth in which drought follows his death, it is most often held that the infertility of the land is a result of the violent nature of his death, since he is murdered. But what is usually overlooked is the fact that Aqhat's death, like the death of Saul's descendants, represents a case of bad death because his body is missing and he cannot be given a proper funeral. The drought may actually be the result of the inability to observe the required funeral ceremonies. Quite significantly, after the drought ensues, Daniel, Aqhat's father, begins a search for the youth's remains in which he is helped by no other than Baal, the god who is incapacitated by the death of Aqhat. Unburied bodies and bones can bring infertility and from this perspective it is possible to assume that the bones of the Passover sacrifice were buried.[241]

---

241.   Perhaps they were placed in an ossuary. Ossuaries were very popular in Judah in times immediately before the second destruction of the temple. Figueras 1983: 7–10.

However, the purpose of their special treatment was no doubt to ensure the preservation of the essence of the god's life and powers. God's death was to be a case of 'good death'. The regeneration of the god's life, on the other hand, did not rest solely upon the bones of the sacrificial animal. It seems that dew also played a significant role despite the fact that in the Bible it is never mentioned in any connection with the festival. But we do find it in connection with many ideas that are also part of the Passover's symbolism and, more directly, as was said before, in a prayer which is part of the festival's synagogue service.

It is hard to discover what was the true nature of the relationship between the divine patron of rain and dew. Both rain and dew were perceived as having life-giving powers and in that capacity they are in the Bible very often mentioned together, as a pair.[242] With respect to Passover, dew might have played a similar role to that of the bones, as the essence of rain, given that it was seen to represent the rain in its purified form.[243] Or perhaps it was comprehended as the rain god's child. Psalm 110.3 speaks about dew as being born, while Job 38.28 characterizes it as begotten. However, there can be little doubt that it indeed played some role in the god's revival since it is associated with the world of the dead and feeding and raising of dead bodies.[244] Psalm 110.3 also hints at its messianic character.[245] In the same capacity we find it in the story about the period of wandering through the wilderness, the period of the symbolic temporary death of the nation, where dew is associated with manna, the food of salvation.[246] In the Exodus version, the impression is that dew itself becomes the miracle food, because manna appears as dew vanishes. The Numbers version is slightly different because here they fall together during the night. In both versions, however, dew and manna ensure the continuance of the nation during its temporary absence and separation from the promized land, the symbolic land of living.

How, when and in which form the god of rain went through the reversal of the forced dormant condition in order to regain his fertilizing, potent form and symbolically return to the world of the living is a question that will have to be left unanswered since there are too many theories that are feasible. The time when his return was expected might have been already during Passover, perhaps on its third day as the Christian tradition suggests. Or at Weeks, when the harvest was over, and as it is suggested by the custom of half mourning during the period of omer counting. Or, during Tabernacles when the rains were expected to gain momentum. He

242. Deut. 32.2; 2 Sam. 1.21; 1 Kgs 17.1; Job 38.28.
243. Deut. 32.2.
244. Isa. 26.19.
245. Garbini 2003: 111.
246. Exod. 16.13–14; Num. 11.9.

might have returned as the young god, as dew, which was consequently supposed to reach maturity by autumn. Or he might have come back in his fully developed form, as the autumnal seasonal rains, fed and maintained by dew during the period of going through the ordeal of passivity.[247]

However, as far as our discussion regarding the symbolic references of Passover's individual elements is concerned, it ends at this point with the conclusion that the special treatment of the bones and the indirect involvement of dew implicitly suggest the idea of return, but also with the realization that for the questions as to when and in which form that latent return was actualized we are in no position to offer a confident interpretation.

Conclusions

This study has pursued several goals in discussing the development and the symbolism of Passover. The first one was to refute the traditional view that Passover was a combination of two originally independent feasts and to establish its pre-commemorative function. The hypothesis about its dual origin has been probed through analysis of various arguments that are put forward in its support and their relation to the biblical texts. The results of the analysis demonstrated that the biblical texts, despite their different representations, preserve the ritual unity of Passover. The only exception was the legislation in Deuteronomy. In contrast to the opinion of the majority of scholars that the centralization was responsible for the fusion of two festivals, it has been established that with respect to Passover's ritual structure the centralizing tendencies reflected in Deuteronomy had a disintegrative effect that in time led to the perception about two festivals. From the discussion regarding its dual origin, Passover appeared as a typical Near Eastern communal fertility festival fundamentally associated with a temple as the place of its observance. The discussion of its place in the calendar further clarified its pre-commemorative purpose as the festival related to the agricultural season in which it took place.

In order to establish its particular pre-commemorative function we had to implement a methodology that would go beyond the Yahwistic ideology in reading the biblical texts concerned with Passover. Proceeding along these lines, we have introduced a structuralist reading of various narrative texts in order to establish the symbolic function of Passover in

247. My personal choice is the Feast of Weeks, given that in the Ugaritic myth, although Baal revives in El's dream, the land is nevertheless parched and the sun god is dispatched to find him which is an indication of an interregnum between the god's revival and the demonstration of that revival. Gibson 1978: 77–78.

the context of Yahwistic ideology, maintaining that symbolism is the bridging link between the old and the new religious ideas. The constants, the binary oppositions and a third mediating agent, which surfaced after the analysis, demonstrated that in the Old Testament an actual celebration of Passover is always mentioned in particular situations, more precisely, between such periods in Israelite history which, according to the mythological pattern of comprehending the world, need reconciliation through a third intermediatory agent whose purpose is to establish a continuity between the two stages. The function of pre-commemorative Passover has been, therefore, established as a ritual of passage.

Building on the idea that rites of passage have a trans-formative, rather than only per-formative character we have proceeded to investigate the symbol system of Passover. From that investigation, the symbolism of Passover emerged as a complexity of interrelated meanings referring to life and death, order and chaos, culture and nature, divine and human, danger and salvation, that are through an intricate interplay of diversity of symbols, such as light, sun, the number seven, night, eating, dew and so on, associated to form its web-like texture.

However, the structural coherence of the discrete meanings of the rituals and acts and their mutual internal logic as consequential parts of a whole became intelligible and transparent only when the idea of harvest was introduced into the centre of this web of the explicit and the implicit. It was found that it was the season of harvest and its restorative character, its realities and the existential anxieties associated with it that defined the meaning of the festival as a whole and each of its individual elements.

The reality context of the season, which commanded the logic behind and among rituals and individual acts and which was reflected in them, was marked by insecurities and fears regarding the possibly detrimental natural conditions with respect to the crops and the outcome of the harvest. Passover began with eating unleavened bread and removal of leaven as simple homeopathic acts to prevent the corruption of the new grains. These acts were followed by preparing the stalks of barley for cutting, which, however, could not be performed before the most significant natural adversary for the success of the harvest that was idiosyncratic for this particular time of the year was effectively removed. The obstacle in question were the rains and their temporary suspension and therefore also removal of their destructive capacities was effected through killing and eating the sacrificial animal, the apotheosized incarnation of the wet season. The completion of this act meant that the last of the safeguards against the failure of the crops was in place and that the final, rewarding stage in the long and arduous process of growing the grains could begin. The subsequent ceremonial cutting of the first sheaves of barley and their presentation in the temple opened the period of harvest. The special treatment of the bones implies that precautions were taken in order to restore the rains in their appointed season but, in general, this is the furthest point of the festival, as it is presented in the Bible, which we are able to reach.

In general terms, the observance of pre-commemorative Passover, as the transitory point towards this enormously important period of harvest, which was expected to renew the vitality of the community, meant life instead of death, order instead of chaos, salvation instead of doom. It was a festival that dealt with basic existential concerns and interests of people that depended on agriculture for their survival.

BIBLIOGRAPHY

Albertz, R.
  1994   *A History of the Israelite Religion in the Old Testament Period* (trans. J. Bowden; London: SCM Press [1992]).

Alexander, T.D.
  1995   'The Passover Sacrifice', in R.T. Beckwith and M.J. Selaman (eds.), *Sacrifice in the Bible* (Carlisle: Paternoster Press; Grand Rapids: Baker Book House): 1–25.

Anderson, B.
  1978   *The Living World of the Old Testament* (London: Longman).

Beer, G.
  1912   *Pesachim (Ostern): Text, Übersetzung und Erklarung* (Giessen: Topelmann).

Bergant, D.
  1995   'An Anthropological Approach to Biblical Interpretation: The Passover Supper in Exodus 12:1–20 as a Case of Study', in Mark McVann (ed.), *Transformations, Passages, and Processes: Ritual Approaches to Biblical Texts* (Semeia, 67; Atlanta: Scholars Press): 43–63.

Blackman, A.M.
  1933   'Myth and Ritual in Ancient Egypt', in S.H. Hooke (ed.), *Myth and Ritual: Essays on the Myth and Ritual of the Hebrews in Relation to the Culture Pattern of the Ancient East* (London: Oxford University Press): 15–39.

Bloch, M., and J. Perry,
  1982   'Introduction: Death and Regeneration of Life', in M. Bloch and J. Perry (eds.), *Death and the Regeneration of Life* (New York: Cambridge University Press): 1–45.

Bokser, B.M.
  1974   *The Origins of Seder: The Passover Rite and Early Rabbinic Judaism* (Berkeley: University of California Press).

Bonanno, A. (ed.)
  1985   *Archeology and Fertility Cult in the Ancient Mediterranean* (Amsterdam: B.R. Grüner Publishing Co.).

Bradshaw, P.F.
  1999   'The Origins of Easter', in P.F. Bradshaw and A. Hofman (eds.), *Passover and Easter: Origin and History to Modern Times* (Two Liturgical Traditions, 5; Notre Dame: University of Indiana): 81–97.

Brumfield, A.C.
  1981   *The Attic Festivals of Demeter and their Relation to the Agricultural Year* (Salem: The Ayer Co.).

Campbell, J.
  1991   *The Masks of God: Primitive Mythology* (Harmondsworth: Arkana [1959]).

Caplan, P.

1992   *Feasts, Fasts, Famine: Food for Thought* (Berg Occasional Papers in Anthropology; Oxford/Providence: Berg).

Carmichael, C.M

1974   *The Laws of Deuteronomy* (Ithaca, NY: Cornell University Press).

Carroll, R.P.

1998   'Exile! What Exile?: Deportation and the Discourses of Diaspora', in L. Grabbe (ed.), *Leading Captivity Captive: 'The Exile' as History and Ideology* (JSOTSup, 278, European Seminar in Historical Methodology, 2; Sheffield: Sheffield Academic Press): 62–79.

Childs, B.S.

1974   *Exodus: A Commentary* (London: SCM Press).

Clines, D.

1998   *On the Way to the Postmodern: Old Testament Essays, 1967–1998* (JSOTSup, 292; 2 vols.; Sheffield: Sheffield Academic Press).

Cohen, M.E.

1993   *The Cultic Calendars of the Ancient Near East* (Betsheda: CDL Press).

Cohn, R.L.

1981   *The Shape of Sacred Space: Essays in Old Testament Religion and Theology* (American Academy of Religion Studies in Religion, 23; Chico, CA: Scholars Press).

Comstock, W.R. (ed.)

1971   *Religion and Man: An Introduction* (New York: Harper & Row).

Coote, R.B., and K.W. Whitelam,

1987   *The Emergence of Early Israel in Historical Perspective* (The Social World of Biblical Antiquity Series; Sheffield: Almond Press).

Cross, F.M.

1973   *Canaanite Myth and Hebrew Epic: Essays in the History of the Religion of Israel* (Cambridge: Harvard University Press).

Davies, J.D.

1997   *Death, Ritual and Belief: The Rhetoric of Funerary Rites* (London: Cassell).

Davies, P.R.

1992   *In Search of 'Ancient Israel'* (JSOT.Sup, 148; Sheffield: Sheffield Academic Press).

Davies-Floyd, R.E.

1992   *Birth as an American Rite of Passage* (Berkeley: University of California Press).

Douglas, M.

1966   *Purity and Danger* (London: Routledge & Kegan Paul).

Eco, Umberto

1989   *The Open Work* (Cambridge: Harvard University Press).

Edelman, D.V. (ed.)

1995   'Introduction', in D.V. Edelman, *The Triumph of Elohim: From Yahwisms to Judaisms* (Kampen: Kok Pharos Publishing House): 15–27.

Eilberg-Schwartz, H.

1990   *The Savage in Judaism: An Anthropology of Israelite Religion and Ancient Judaism* (Bloomington: Indiana University Press).

Eliade, M
    1954   *The Myth of the Eternal Return or Cosmos and History* (trans. W.R. Trask; Billingen Series, 46; Princeton: Princeton University Press).
    1959   *The Sacred and the Profane: The Nature of Religion* (trans. W.R. Trask; New York and London: Harcourt Brace Jovanovich).

Engnell, I.
    1952   'Paesah-Massot and the Problem of "Paternism"', *Orientalia Suecana* 1: 39–50.
    1970   *Critical Essays on the Old Testament* (London: SPCK).

Figueras, P.
    1983   *Decorated Jewish Ossuaries* (Leiden: Brill).

Finegan, J.
    1964   *Handbook of Biblical Chronology: Principles of Time Reckoning in the Ancient World and Problems of Chronology in the Bible. (Princeton: Princeton University Press).*

Fishbane, M.
    1985   *Biblical Interpretation in Ancient Israel* (Oxford: Clarendon Press).

Flavius, Josephus
    1927   *Jewish Antiquities* (trans. H. St. J. Thackeray; Cambridge: Harvard University Press London: Heinemann,).
    1927   *The Jewish War* (trans. H. St. J. Thackeray; Cambridge: Harvard University Press London: Heinemann).

Fohrer, G.
    1973   *History of Israelite Religion* (London: SPCK).

Frazer, J.G.
    1914   *The Golden Bough: A Study in Magic and Religion.* IV. *Adonis Attis Osiris* (London: Macmillan).

Frye, N.
    1982   *The Great Code: The Bible and Literature* (London: Routledge & Kegan Paul).

Garbini, G.
    1988   *History and Ideology in Ancient Israel* (New York: Crossroad).
    2003   *Myth and History in the Bible* (JSOTSup, 362; Sheffield: Sheffield Academic Press).

Gaster, T.H.
    1958   *Passover: Its History and Traditions* (London and New York: Abelard–Schuman).
    1975   *Thespis: Ritual, Myth, and Drama in the Ancient Near East* (New York: Gordian Press, rev. edn).

Gehlen, A.
    1988   *Man, his Nature and Place in the World* (New York: Columbia University Press [1950]).

Gennep, A. van
    1960   *The Rites of Passage* (trans. M.B. Vizedom and G.L. Caffee; Chicago: University of Chicago Press [1908]).

Gibson, J. (ed.)
    1978   *Canaanite Myths and Legends* (Edinburgh: T. & T. Clark [originally edited by G.R. Driver] [1956]).

Ginsberg, L.H.
    1982   *Israelian Heritage* (New York: KTAV Publishing House).
Goldziher, I.
    1967   *Mythology Among the Hebrews and Its Historical Development* (trans. R. Martineau; New York: Cooper Square Press [1877]).
Goodenough, E.R.
    1988   *Jewish Symbols in the Greco-Roman Period* (Bolingen Series; Princeton: Princeton University Press, Bolingen Series, abridged edn).
Gorman, F.H., Jr.
    1990   *The Ideology of Ritual: Space, Time and Status in the Priestly Theology* (JSOTSup, 91: Sheffield: Sheffield Academic Press).
Gottwald, N.K.
    1993   *The Hebrew Bible in Its Social World and Ours* (Atlanta: Scholars Press).
Goudoever, J. van
    1961   *Biblical Calendars* (Leiden: Brill).
Grainger, R.
    1974   *The Language of the Rite* (London: Darton, Longman & Todd).
Gray, G.B.
    1925   *Sacrifice in the Old Testament: Its Theory and Practice* (New York: KTAV Publishing House; repr. 1971).
Grimes, R.L.
    2000   *Deeply into the Bone: Re-inventing Rites of Passage* (Berkeley: University of California Press).
Haran, M.
    1985   *Temples and Temple-Service in Ancient Israel: An Inquiry into Biblical Cult Phenomena and the Historical Setting of the Priestly School* (Winona Lake: Eisenbrauns).
Harris L.R., L.A. Gleason Jr. and B.K. Waltke
    1980   *Theological Wordbook of the Old Testament* (Chicago: Moody Bible Institute).
Hertz, R.
    1960   'A Contribution to the Study of Collective Representation of Death', in R. Needham and C. Needham (eds.), *Death and the Right Hand* (New York: Free Press [1906]): 27–86.
James, E.O.
    1961   *Seasonal Feasts and Festivals* (London: Thames & Hudson).
    1962   *The Ancient Gods: The History and Diffusion of Religion in the Ancient Near East and Eastern Mediterranean* (London: Readers Union).
Johnstone, W.
    1990   *Exodus* (Sheffield: Sheffield Academic Press).
Joseph, N.
    1986   *Uniforms and Nonuniforms: Communication Through Clothing* (Contributions in Sociology, 61; New York: Greenwood Press).
Kaufmann, Y.
    1961   *The Religion of Israel: From its Beginnings to the Babylonian Exile* (trans. M. Greenberg; London: George Allen & Unwin).
Keel, O. and C. Uehlinger
    1998   *Gods, Goddesses and Images of Gods in Ancient Israel* (Minneapolis: Fortress).

Keesing, R.M.
> 1975 *Cultural Anthropology: A Contemporary Perspective* (Chicago: Reinhard and Winston Inc.).

Kraus, H.J.
> 1966 *Worship in Israel: A Cultic History of the Old Testament* (Oxford: Blackwell).

Langdon, S. (ed.)
> 1933 *Babylonian Menologies and the Semitic Calendar* (London: Oxford University Press).

Leach, E.
> 1969 *Genesis as Myth and Other Essays* (London: Jonathan Cape).
> 1980 'Anthropological Approaches to the Bible during the Twentieth Century', in G. Tucker and D. Knight (eds.), *Humanizing America's Iconic Book* (Chico: Scholars Press): 75–94.

Leach E., and A.D. Aycock
> 1983 *Structuralist Interpretation of Biblical Myth* (Cambridge: Cambridge University Press/Royal Anthropological Institute of Great Britain and Ireland).

Leeuw, G. van der
> 1963 *Religion in Essence and Manifestation: A Study in Phenomenology* (trans. J.E. Turner; 2 vols.; repr. New York and Evanston: Harper & Row [1938]).

Lemche, N.P.
> 1988 *Ancient Israel: A New History of Israelite Society* (Sheffield: JSOT Press).
> 1993 'The Old Testament – A Hellenistic Book?', *Scandinavian Journal of the Old Testament* 7: 163–93.
> 1997 'Clio is also among the Muses! Keith W. Whitelam and the History of Palestine: A Review and Commentary', in L.L. Grabbe (ed.), *Can a 'History of Israel' Be Written?* (JSOTSup, 245, European Seminar in Historical Methodology, 1; Sheffield: Sheffield Academic Press): 123–56.

Levenson, J.D.
> 1993 *The Death and the Resurrection of the Beloved Son: The Transformation of Child Sacrifice in Judaism and Christianity* (New Haven: Yale University Press).

Levinson, B.M.
> 1997 *Deuteronomy and the Hermeneutics of the Legal Innovation* (Oxford and New York: Oxford University Press).

Levi-Strauss, C.
> 1955 'The Structural Study of Myth', in T.A. Sebeok (ed.), *Myth: A Symposium* (Bloomington: Indiana University Press): 81–106.

May, H.G.
> 1936 'The Relation of the Passover to the Festival of Unleavened Cakes', *Journal of Biblical Literature* 4: 65.

McConville, J.G.
> 1984 *Law and Theology in Deuteronomy* (Sheffield: JSOT Press).

Mettinger, T.N.D.
> 2001 *The Riddle of Resurrection : 'Dying and Rising Gods' in the Ancient Near East* (Stockholm: Almqvist & Wiksell International).

Moor, J. de
    1972   *New Year with Canaanites and Israelites* (2 vols;. Kampen: Kok).
Mowinckel, S.
    1922   *Psalmenstudien*, II. (Oslo: Kristiania).
Nakanose, S.
    1993   *Josiah's Passover: Sociology and the Liberating Bible* (New York: Orbis Books).
Neusner, Jacob (trans.)
    1988   *The Mishnah* (New Haven: Yale University Press).
Nicolsky, N.M.
    1927   'Pascha im Kulte des Jerusalemischen Temples', *Zeitschrift für die alttesta-mentliche Wissenschaft* 14: 171–241.
Nilsson, M.P.
    1920   *Primitive Time-Reckoning: A Study in the Origins and First Development of the Art of Counting Time Among Primitive and Early Culture* (Lund: Gleerup).
Noth, M.
    1962   *Exodus: A Commentary* (trans. J.S. Bowden; London: SCM Press).
Nulman, M.
    1993   *The Encyclopedia of Jewish Prayer* (London: Jason Aronson Inc.).
Olmo Lete, G. del
    1999   *Canaanite Religion: According to the Liturgical Texts of Ugarit* (Betsheda: CDL Press).
Pallis, S.A.
    1926   *The Babylonian Akitu Festival* (Copenhagen: Hovedkommissionaer: A. F. Høst).
Pedersen, J.
    1959   *Israel: Its Life and Culture,* III-IV (London: Oxford University Press [1925]).
Philo
    1929–62   *Works,* I-X (trans. F.H. Colson; Loeb Classical Library; London: Heinemann; Cambridge: Harvard University Press).
Pierce, J.M.
    1999   'Holy Week and Easter in the Middle Ages', in P.F. Bradshaw and A. Hofman (eds.), *Passover and Easter: Origin and History to Modern Times* (Two Liturgical Traditions, 5; Notre Dame: University of Indiana): 161–89.
Pritchard, James B. (ed.)
    1969   *Ancient Near Eastern Texts: Relating to the Old Testament* (Princeton: Princeton University Press, 3rd edn with supplements).
Ringgren, H.
    1969   *Israelite Religion* (trans. D. Green; London: SPCK).
Roach, M.E., and J.B. Eicher
    1979   'The Language of Personal Adornment', in J.M. Cordwell and R.M. Schwartz (eds.), *The Fabrics of Culture: The Anthropology of Clothing and Adornment* (The Hague: Mouton Publishers): 7–21.
Rooy, H.F. van
    1985   'Fertility as Blessing and Infertility as Curse in the Ancient Near East and the Old Testament', in A. Bonanno (ed.), *Archeology and Fertility Cult in the Ancient Mediterranean* (Amsterdam: B.R. Grüner Publishing Co.): 225–35.

Sarna, N.
    1986   *Exploring Exodus: The Heritage of Biblical Israel* (New York: Schocken Books).

Schmid, H.H.
    1976   *Der sogenannte Jahwist. Beobachtungen und Fragen zur Pentateuchforschung* (Zurich: Theologischer Verlag).

Segal, J.B.
    1963   *The Hebrew Passover: From the Earliest Times to A.D. 70* (London Oriental Series, 12; London: Oxford University Press).

Sen, A.
    1976   'Famines as Failures of Exchange Entitlements', *Economic and Political Weekly of Bombay* 11 (special number).

Seters, J. van
    1975   *Abraham in History and Tradition* (New Haven: Yale University Press).
    1983   'The Place of the Yahwist in the History of Passover and Massot', *Zeitschrift für die alttestamentliche Wissenschaft* 95: 167–81.

Smith, D.L.
    1989   *The Religion of the Landless: The Social Context of the Babylonian Exile* (Bloomington: Meyer-Stone Books).

Smith, J.Z.
    1987   *To Take Place: Toward Theory of Ritual* (Chicago: University of Chicago Press).

Smith, M.S.
    2001   *The Origins of Biblical Monotheism: Israel's Polytheistic Background and the Ugaritic Texts* (Oxford: Oxford University Press).

Smith, P.
    1982   'Aspects of the Organization of Rites', in M. Izard and P. Smith (eds.), *Between Belief and Transgression: Structuralist Essays in Religion, History and Myth* (trans. J. Leavittand; Chicago: University of Chicago Press): 103–128.

Smith, R.J.
    1907   *Lectures on the Religion of the Semites* (London: Adam and Charles Black, rev. edn).

Snaith, N.H.
    1947   *The Jewish New Year Festival: Its Origins and Development* (London: SPCK).

Stevenson, K.
    1988   *Jerusalem Revisited: The Liturgical Meaning of Holy Week* (Washington: Pastoral Press).

Talmon, S.
    1976   'Wilderness', *Interpreter's Dictionary of Bible*, Supplementary Volume.

Tawil, H.
    1980   'Azazel the Prince of the Steepe: A Comparative Study', *Zeitschrift für die alttestamentliche Wissenschaft* 92: 43–59.

Thompson, T.L.
    1994   *Early History of the Israelite People: From the Written and Archaeological Sources* (Leiden: E.J. Brill).
    1995   'The Intellectual Matrix of Early Biblical Narrative: Inclusive Monotheism in Persian Period Palestine', in D.V. Edelman (ed.), *The Triumph of Elohim:*

From Yahwisms to Judaisms (Kampen: Kok Pharos Publishing House): 107–127.

1997   'Defining History and Ethnicity in the South Levant', in L.L. Grabbe (ed.), *Can a 'History of Israel' Be Written?* (JSOTSup, 245, European Seminar in Historical Methodology, 1; Sheffield: Sheffield Academic Press): 166–88.

1999   *The Bible in History: How Writers Create a Past* (London: Jonathan Cape).

Tigay, J.H.

1996   *Deuteronomy* (The JPS Torah Commentary; Philadelphia: The Jewish Publication Society).

Toorn, K. van der

1992   'Anat-Yahu, Some Other Deities, and the Jews of Elephantine', *Numen* 39 (April): 80–101.

2002   'Israelite Figurines: A View from the Texts', in B.M. Gittlen (ed.), *Sacred Time, Sacred Space* (Winona Lake: Eisenbrauns): 45–63.

Turner, V.W.

1974   *Dramas, Fields and Metaphors* (Ithaca, NY: Cornell University Press).

1977   'Symbols in African Rituals', in J.L. Dolgin, D.S. Kemnitzer and D.M. Schneider (eds.), *Symbolic Anthropology: A Reader in the Study of Symbols and Meanings* (New York: Columbia University Press): 183–94.

1979   *The Ritual Process: Stucture and Antistructure* (Ithaca, NY: Cornell University Press [1969]).

Vaux, Roland de

1965   *Ancient Israel*, I, II (2 vols.; New York: McGraw-Hill).

1978   *The Early History of Israel* (trans. D. Smith; Philadelphia: Westminster Press).

Weinfeld, M.

1972   *Deuteronomy and the Deuteronomic School* (Oxford: Oxford University Press).

Wellhausen, J.

1885   *Prolegomena to the History of Israel* (trans. J. Sutherland Black and A. Menzies; Edinburgh: A&C Black).

Werbulowsky, R.J.Z., and G. Wigoder (eds.)

1967   *The Encyclopedia of the Jewish Religion* (Jerusalem: Masada Press).

Wyatt, N.

2000   *Serving the Gods* (Sheffield: Sheffield Academic Press).

Zareen-Zohar, E.

1999   'From Passover to Shavuot', in P.F. Bradshaw and A.L. Hofman (eds.), *Passover and Easter: The Symbolic Structuring of Sacred Seasons* (Two Liturgical Traditions, 6; Notre Dame: University of Indiana): 71–94.

Zeitlin, I.M.

1984   *Ancient Judaism: Biblical Criticism from Max Weber to the Present* (New York: Polity Press).

Zevit, Z.

2001   *The Religions of Ancient Israel: A Synthesis of Parallactic Approaches* (London: Continuum).

INDEX OF REFERENCES

BIBLE